17 , 19 , 90 , 125 , 129 , 146 , 148 , 152 , 153

THOMAS JEFFERSON AND HIS LIBRARY

THOMAS JEFFERSON
AND HIS LIBRARY

A Study of His Literary Interests
and of the Religious Attitudes
Revealed by Relevant Titles
in His Library

BY CHARLES B. SANFORD

ARCHON BOOKS / 1977

Library of Congress Cataloging in Publication Data

Sanford, Charles B
  Thomas Jefferson and his library.

  Bibliography: p.
  Includes index.
    1. Jefferson, Thomas, Pres. U. S., 1743-1826—Books
and reading.   2. Jefferson, Thomas, Pres. U. S., 1743-1826—
Religion.   3. United States. Library of Congress. Jefferson
Collection.   4. Jefferson, Thomas, Pres. U. S., 1743-1826—
Library.   I. Title.
E332.2S26   973.4'6'0924   77-2147
ISBN 0-208-01629-5

© Charles B. Sanford 1977

First published 1977 as an Archon Book,

an imprint of The Shoe String Press, Inc.

Hamden, Connecticut 06514

Printed in the United States of America

Contents

[5]

Tables

[6]

Preface

THOMAS JEFFERSON has long intrigued scholars. He was a man
of wide interests who wrote extensively on many subjects; hence,
there is ample material of his intellectual pursuits to engage a
researcher. He was a complex personality, reticent about his
personal life; so there is plenty of room for those elements of
interpretation and disagreement in which scholars delight.
Jefferson is important not only for shaping the events of a vital
period of history but also for foreshadowing many of the issues
of our times.

It is unfortunate, however, that scholars have tended to study
divergent aspects of his genius separately. Some have seen
him as a politician and statesman and have chronicled his life
in terms of the offices he held. Some classical scholars have seen
Jefferson as a classical student. Students of architecture have
seen Jefferson as an architect. Some women authors have sought
to examine Jefferson's family life and women friends, and some
librarians have studied Jefferson's libraries. Far too little attention has been given to trying to use the knowledge and insight
gained from the varied researches into the life and person of
Thomas Jefferson and the ample Jeffersonian material in a
unified approach. It seems particularly unfortunate that bibliographic essays about Jefferson's books and studies of his libraries
have not been utilized for biographical and historical insights
concerning Jefferson himself. For men of many intellectual

interests like Jefferson, it is in the inner life of the mind and
spirit that the key to their lives and actions is to be found, and
it is in the library record of their reading interests that the intellectual life may be studied. This conviction is the basis of the
present study.

The method of this study has been to analyze the holdings
of Jefferson's library to determine its focus and emphases, in
order to note Jefferson's main interests. Conclusions concerning
Jefferson's reading interests as indicated by his library holdings
were checked against Jefferson's writings. Jefferson's interests
and library emphases have been studied further by comparing
them with those of other contemporary libraries.

Jefferson's own writings are quoted extensively for the reader's
convenience, since the material about Jefferson is scattered in
many sources. Jefferson's ideas are to be found in a wide variety
of letters, speeches, documents, and short essays discussing
many subjects, and rarely in a long polished work. His writings
are poorly indexed and difficult to locate. Most researchers
tend to use a few documents bearing on their subject without
locating many other minor statements scattered throughout
Jefferson's writings. It is unfortunate that the project to gather
together, index, and publish all the Jeffersonian material begun
by Julian Boyd at Princeton[1] has not been completed.

The special focus for this study of Jefferson's reading interests
is his religious, ethical, and philosophical ideas. Scholars have
given much less attention to these interests of Jefferson than to
studies devoted to his political and social beliefs. In the past,
many writings about Jefferson's religion have been partisan,
and there is need for more comprehensive and more objective
study of Jefferson's religious thought and influence.

Besides the few published studies and short articles on various
aspects of Jefferson's religious and philosophical ideas which
have been used and cited in this study, a few unpublished theses
provide useful information. M. Rosaleen Trainor has studied
Jefferson's ideas of human conscience, relating it to his ideas
of freedom of religion and to the background of Catholic
tradition. Constance Bartlett Schulz has contrasted the religious
thought of Jefferson with John Adams, a suggestive comparison,
but her treatment has been necessarily limited. Kenneth Raynor
Williams made his study on the ethics of Jefferson, but his pri-

mary emphasis was on Jefferson's study of ethics as applied to society, government, and such social institutions as the church. Other works a bit farther afield are Reginald Stuart's study of Jefferson's ideas about war and Burton Spivak's study of Jefferson and the embargo.[2]

On the subject of Jefferson and his library, besides the few short published articles and lectures cited, William Peden's dissertation on Jefferson's library building activities and the subject emphases of his library and James Servies's thesis on Jefferson's libraries and his work in the field of subject classification[3] proved helpful.

No studies of Jefferson's reading interests were listed for any of the years of research covered in *Dissertations Abstracts*.[4] Very few studies, in fact, of the influence of books and libraries upon people are to be found. Occasional studies of reading influences on literary or theological figures, along with some studies of the interests of frontier groups in America, are recorded, but none for important historical leaders who were making the decisions for society. Such studies would be helpful adjuncts to modern historical research.

Acknowledgment should be made to the Department of Library Science of the University of Wisconsin-Oshkosh, particularly to Professors Norma Jones and Redmond Burke for suggestions and help in pursuing this study and to the university library, Miss Helen Wahoski, director, and the staff for freely making all their holdings available, and to Librarian Gerald Carpenter for diligently obtaining rare materials by interlibrary loan.

1

Libraries and History

As STANLEY PARGELLIS of the Newberry Library has noted, "Librarians . . . tend to be systematizers, . . . counters, planners, standardizers, fomenters of vast projects, disregarders of men and women as individuals and interested only in mankind—and books—in the mass . . . unhistorically minded." He compares them to "butterflies whose span of existence is compressed into hours between sunup and sunset [thinking] in terms of the fleeting present only but seldom with any sense of the past from which both present and future spring."[1] By lacking an awareness of librarianship's roots in a great tradition from ancient, Renaissance, and early public libraries, the modern librarian, in his busy concern for many things, loses a sense that he has a part in laying "another stone in the great temple of knowledge."[2] He is the poorer for it.

Society also is the poorer for its neglect of library history. Louis Shores, in an article presented to the 1947 American Library Association Conference, wrote:

> If . . . history [is] the story of man's past and [the] attempt to preserve the records of civilization, then the negligence of librarianship approaches a professional misdeameanor. How can we assume responsibility for the dissemination of these records and at the same time suppress through procrastination an important segment

of them? If institutions constitute a significant phase of historical study, then which single institutional type can have greater importance to the story of man's past than the repositories of the record?[3]

In the earlier years of library research the library was studied largely as a separate entity. Histories of individual libraries were written and attempts were made to trace their early beginnings, such as Austin Keep's study of the colonial beginnings of the New York Public Library in 1909, often with the hope of proving that one's own was the earliest library.[4]

In more recent times there has come a recognition that public libraries do not develop by themselves but as a part of the society they serve. Thus, Jesse Shera concludes his study of the growth of the public library movement from the intellectual and cultural conditions of New England:

> Judged by every standard and measured by every criterion, the public library is revealed as a social agency dependent upon the objectives of society. It *followed*—it did not create—social change. It was an outward and visible manifestation of the spirit and ideals of the people. Borne on the rising tide of modern democracy, it evolved as society itself developed, though at a somewhat slower pace. As society attained greater complexity, as industry developed and increased in diversity, as populations crowded into congested city areas, as labor and economic life, largely because of the impact of the machine, became more and more specialized, the functions of the library reflected a corresponding intricacy and growing importance.[5]

James Hart reached somewhat similar conclusions in his study of the "popular book." He has taken the best-sellers of different periods of American history and interpreted their success as meeting certain social and cultural needs of the moment. He found Bunyan's *Pilgrim's Progress* successful, for example, because it was an exciting tale, told from the Puritan religious viewpoint, understandable to the naive, and suited to New England life. Even more popular was a forgotten little "pocket size, practical guide to life and religion which

summarized doctrine, . . . contrasted the regenerate and unre-
generate man . . . and was a good antidote to witchcraft. With
it any reader could deal with God and . . . all would work
out well."[6]

The library, with its records of reading tastes and interests,
thus has come to be recognized as an important source of material
for studying society, and as a mirror that faithfully reflects the
interests, concerns, beliefs, and issues that agitate people. Too
little use has been made in the past of this rich resource for
historical and social research.

Does the library, however, do no more than reflect society?
Does it not also help shape society by its educational and cultural influences? Shera gives some suggestion of this influence:

> There was a lag between social stimulus and literary
> response, yet there also existed a reciprocity of relation-
> ship between the library and society. Each reacted upon
> the other. Because the public library contributed to the
> fullest expression of democracy, it supported that form
> of social organization. The relationship was constantly
> evolving.[7]

However, he goes back to his primary emphasis upon the
socially dependent nature of American libraries:

> If future generations can learn anything from an exam-
> ination of library history, it is that the objectives of the
> public library are directly dependent upon the objectives
> of society itself. The true frame of reference for the library
> is to be found in its coeval culture.[8]

It is the thesis of this study that books and libraries do more
than reflect individual interests and social needs. They also
affect individual beliefs and social action. They are, therefore,
important sources of primary historical data, along with deeds,
wills, and diaries, that historians have often overlooked.

A good example of the effective use of library materials for
historical research was the masterful study which Samuel Elliot
Morrison did of the Puritan character by using early library
records including wills, sermons, school curricula, and book-

sellers' order lists as evidence to disprove the popular notion
that the Puritans were uneducated lower-class bigots.[9]

Elmer Johnson, in his *History of Libraries in the Western
World*, has also recognized the effect of libraries upon history:

> Many colonial Americans were not even literate, much
> less interested in literature, but surprisingly large numbers
> of them did own and read books. In particular, those who
> emerged as political and social leaders usually owned books
> or had access to them, and indeed many of them had well-
> selected private libraries. It has been estimated that Phila-
> delphia had as many libraries and bookstores in 1760 as
> any European city of comparable size. Moreover, the
> colonial leaders not only owned books but read them, and
> with considerable taste. From their own private libraries
> and from the bookstores of the coastal towns or their mer-
> chants in England, they had access to almost any book
> available for sale in Europe at that time. That they made
> effective use of them is evidenced in the Declaration of
> Independence, the Constitution of the United States, and
> the numerous journals, diaries, letters and books that have
> come down to us from the colonial era.[10]

While it may be true that we read books because we have an
interest or inclination toward them, it is also true that what
we read subtly and cumulatively influences us. An individual
library and librarian can not advance too far beyond the beliefs
and perhaps prejudices of the society that supports them. Never-
theless the books that are written and published, are selected
by bookmen and librarians, and then are reviewed, read, and
discussed, help mold public opinion; and in a free democracy
public opinion helps to make history.

The war in Vietnam is a modern example. In a few short
years this war, which was generally accepted by the American
people under the leadership of Presidents Eisenhower and
Kennedy as a crusade to stop communism and save freedom in
southeast Asia, became an immoral war waged by degenerate
America against a valiant small nation, North Vietnam. This
change in public opinion will be utterly incomprehensible to
future historians until they study the books and periodical

articles on the subject in our libraries and the videotapes of the tv news programs of the period which had such a large influence in creating these changed attitudes.

The present study is undertaken in the conviction that by studying the books and libraries of important leaders of the past, insight can be gained into the thinking which affected their actions and shaped history. New light is shed upon history by studying the sources of the ideas that shaped it, as seen in the reading of important leaders.

Thomas Jefferson: a Case Study in Library History

Thomas Jefferson seems a happy choice for a bibliographic-historical study for two reasons: (1) he was an important historic figure who left voluminous primary source material in his letters and writings, and (2) by a fortunate accident of history, an accurate and extensive record of his library holdings and his readings has been preserved. This study examines Jefferson's interest in books and the libraries that he spent his life collecting. An analysis is made of Jefferson's library holdings to discover his literary interests, and a comparison made with the library holdings and interests of other colonial leaders and collectors. The particular scope of this study is Jefferson's religion. A detailed study of the particular titles in Jefferson's library dealing with philosophy, ethics, and religion is given, and conclusions drawn contrasting the religious interests and beliefs revealed by these titles with the religious beliefs and interests revealed in Jefferson's own writings.

There are in Jefferson's writings and in his traits of character striking contradictions that long have puzzled scholars. He was an aristocrat who championed the rights of the common man, a wealthy slave owner who opposed the institution of slavery, a piously reared youth who wrote some harsh criticisms of religion, and a free-thinking deist who wrote two books on religion. He was a plantation owner who worked with his slaves in agriculture and building, a scholar of the classics who was an inveterate inventor, a diplomat, at home in the courts of Europe, who led his country in an isolationist foreign policy. It is this writer's belief that it is only by studying the intellectual history of Thomas Jefferson, the influence his studies and reading had upon his developing thought and beliefs as recorded in both his writings and his library, that these contradictions can be explained. Such a study of literary influences would be as helpful to scholars of Jefferson's political convictions and career as it has been for this study of Jefferson's intellectual and religious life.

2

Thomas Jefferson, Librarian

Jefferson's Interest in Books and Libraries

DESPITE THE tremendous number of volumes that have been published about the life and thought of Thomas Jefferson, comparatively few studies have been made of Jefferson's library interests and activities,[1] and many of these studies have been in the nature of short reviews.[2] Most writers interested in Jefferson's intellectual interests, however, have noted, in passing, his lifelong interest in collecting and studying books and arranging and classifying book collections into libraries.[3]

Jefferson's Love of Reading. All of his life Jefferson was fond of reading, especially of serious reading and studying. His college commonplace books in which he copies favorite passages indicate an early interest in poetry and literature and he always retained his interest in classical epic poetry and Greek drama,[4] but his real interest in books was to use them as a means of serious investigation into important subjects. He had a low opinion of reading fiction.[5]

Evidence of Jefferson's interest in studying is seen in the fact that one of the first items of note he mentions in his *Autobiography* is the schooling he received "at the English school at five years of age, and at the Latin at nine, where I continued . . . with the Reverend Mr. Maury, a correct classical scholar." In 1760, Jefferson continued, he went to William and Mary College, where "it was my great good fortune and . . . probably fixed the destinies of my life . . . [to be guided and taught by] Dr. William Small of Scotland, . . . Professor of Mathematics, . . . science, . . . and the philosophical chair."[6]

Jefferson was clearly stimulated by the exciting vistas of human knowledge and learning that his readings and discussion with his teachers and fellow students opened up to him. Looking back upon his youthful enthusiasm for truth when reviewing his student's notes on common law many years later, Jefferson commented:

> They were written at a time of life when I was bold in the pursuit of knowledge, never fearing to follow truth and reason to whatever results they led, and bearding every authority which stood in their way.[7]

Shortly after completing his study of law with George Wythe, Jefferson outlined his recommended regime of study to a beginning law student. It began with several hours of reading natural science, ethics, and natural religion before eight o'clock, four hours of studying law until noon, an hour of studying books on politics and economics, and the rest of the afternoon reading "the Greek and Latin originals" in ancient history and the works of English and American history. In the evening one should relax by reading "Belle-Lettres," such as the poetry of Milton, the oratory of Cicero, or the drama of Shakespeare.[8] Karl Lehmann comments:

> All in all, it amounts to at least eleven hours of study and reading. It is hard for us to imagine that it could be done day after day for several years. . . . But that Thomas Jefferson did it, at least for some time is unquestionable.[9]

Jefferson remained grateful all his life for the delights of reading and study that his early teachers gave him. In discussing university education with his friend Joseph Priestley, Jefferson wrote:

> To read the Latin and Greek authors in their original, is a sublime luxury. . . . I enjoy Homer in his own language

[18]

infinitely beyond Pope's translation of him, . . . and it is
an innocent enjoyment. I thank on my knees, Him who
directed my early education, for having put into my possession this rich source of delight; and I would not exchange
it for anything which I could then have acquired, and have
not since acquired.[10]

Jefferson repeated his high valuation of the "elegant . . . luxury
of reading the Greek and Roman authors in all the beauties of
their originals" in writing to John Brazier on the importance
of a classical education,[11] and added a sincere tribute to his
father who had first placed Jefferson in school and made provision for his education. Jefferson's father died before the son
entered William and Mary. Jefferson wrote:

I think myself more indebted to my father for this [classical
learning] than for all the other luxuries his cares and affec-
tions have placed within my reach.[12]

Jefferson continued to read and study after he had completed
his formal education. Isaac Jefferson, one of the best workman
of the slaves at Monticello, recalled that Jefferson would often
consult his many books when asked questions about farming
or building. Jefferson, in his enthusiasm, might have twenty
or more books about on the library floor and he would "read
first one then tother."[13] Jefferson would be just as apt to find
answers about farming in his books by Horace as in modern books.
Another illustration of Jefferson's love of reading during his
mature years when he was building Monticello comes from the
account given by the Marquis de Chastellux, a visitor from
France to Jefferson's mountain-top home. In the evening after
dinner and after the women had retired, Chastellux related,

our conversation turned on the poems of Ossian. It was a
spark of electricity which passed rapidly from one to the
other; we recollected the passages in those sublime poems
which particularly struck us. . . . In our enthusiasm the
book was sent for, and placed near the . . . punch bowl,
where, by their mutual aid, the night imperceptibly advanced
upon us.[14]

Jefferson's continued reading and study was not only a delight for him in his early mature years but an excellent preparation for his life of public service. Dumas Malone, Jefferson's most definitive biographer, comments:

> He collected books not merely to own but to use them, and for the same purpose he assiduously assembled ideas and information in his capacious head. He had a rich and ordered storehouse to draw on when . . . he turned his attention again to affairs of state. Also, he was thoroughly prepared for the wise men of Europe when at last the opportunity for learned conversation with them came.[15]

As Jefferson grew busier with the duties of work and the cares of public office, he had less time to indulge his love of reading, although he continued to peruse and purchase books. While in France he spent many happy hours in book stores.[16] While president of the United States, he spent time making a critical study of the New Testament as recreation after the day's work was over.[17] One of Jefferson's youngest granddaughters recalled the encouragement for reading, collecting, preserving information that she received from her grandfather:

> Whenever an opportunity occurred, he sent us books, and he never saw a little story or piece of poetry in a newspaper suited to our ages and tastes, that he did not preserve it and send it to us; and from him we learnt the habit of making . . . collections by pasting in a little paper book made for the purpose, anything of the sort that we received from him or got otherwise.[18]

One of the joys that Jefferson eagerly looked forward to in his retirement from active work was that of having time for reading and study.

> I was a hard student until I entered on the business of life, the duties of which leave no idle time to those disposed to fulfill them; and now, retired, and at the age of seventy-six, I am again a hard student. Indeed, my fondness for reading and study revolts me from the drudgery of letter writing.

. . . I never go to bed without an hour's . . . reading of something moral. . . . I rise with the sun. I use spectacles at night, but not necessarily in the day, unless reading fine print. . . . I enjoy good health.[19]

To his old friend Charles Thomson, Jefferson also wrote of his ability to read usually without glasses and of his wish to have more time for reading, instead of having so much correspondence to answer:

This [correspondence] keeps me at the drudgery of the writing-table all the prime hours of the day, leaving for the gratification of my appetite for reading, only what I can steal from the hours of sleep. Could I reduce this epistolary corvee . . . and give the time redeemed from it to reading and reflection, to history, ethics, mathematics, my life would be as happy as the infirmities of old age would admit.[20]

Although Jefferson occasionally discussed political events and present history with old friends after he retired, he quite evidently was glad to leave the tumult and conflict of the political arena for the serenity of retirement. He cherished the opportunity to read on other than political issues:

I enjoy good health and spirits, and am as industrious a reader as when a student at college. Not of newspapers. These I have discarded. I relinquish, as I ought to do, all intermeddling with public affairs, committing myself cheerfully to the watch and care of those for whom, in my turn, I have watched and cared.[21]

One of Jefferson's grandchildren wrote of the pleasure Jefferson derived from his reading during his retirement.

His love of reading alone . . . made leisure and retirement delightful to him. Books were at all times his chosen companions, and his acquaintance with many languages gave him great power of selection. . . . I saw him more frequently with a volume of the classics in his hand than with any other book. Still he read new publications as they came

out, never missed the new number of a review, especially
of the Edinburgh, and kept himself acquainted with what
was being done, said, or thought in the world from which
he had retired.[22]

Jefferson himself referred to the pleasure he derived from reading
during his retirement in his conversations with John Adams in
which he wrote, "Reading is my delight."[23] In another letter
to Adams, Jefferson wrote of his "canine appetite for reading"
and the way reading was "a lamp to lighten my path."

> My repugnance to the writing table becomes daily and
> hourly more deadly and insurmountable. In place of this
> has come on a canine appetite for reading. And I indulge
> it: because I see in it a relief against the taedium senectutis
> ["weariness of old age"]; a lamp to lighten my path thro'
> the dreary wilderness of time before me, whose bourne
> I see not. Losing daily all interest in the things around us,
> something else is necessary to fill the void. With me it is
> reading, which occupies the mind without the labor of
> producing ideas from my own stock.[24]

Jefferson's mention of his love of reading led Adams to boast
in a friendly way of how much he was also studying in his retirement. Jefferson replied:

> Your undertaking the twelve volumes of Dupuis is a
> degree of heroism to which I could not have aspired even
> in my younger days. I have been contented with the humble
> achievement of reading the Analysis of his work by Destutt-
> Tracy in two hundred pages octavo.[25]

The mention of the work led to a discussion of its ideas, a promise
by Jefferson to send Adams a copy of the book, and to a comment
which reveals Jefferson's methodical library practices:

> I have said to you that it was written by Tracy; and I have
> so entered it on the title-page, as I usually do on Anonymous
> works whose authors are known to me. But Tracy has

requested me not to betray his anonyme, for reasons which may not yet perhaps have ceased to weigh.[26]

In an apology for having not read further on the subject, Jefferson wrote, "I have not entirely read [Tracy's latest work] because I am not fond of reading what is merely abstract, and unapplied immediately to some useful science."[27] One of the greatest pleasures Adams and Jefferson derived from their correspondence in their old age was the opportunity to discuss their reading with each other. They shared their reactions to various works they were reading, and Adams frequently asked Jefferson for information on different subjects and authors.[28]

Jefferson also mentioned his love of reading to other friends. He wrote of it to Abigail Adams and, in paying his respects to John Adams' wife, mentioned a discussion of reading with Benjamin Franklin:

> I am become proprietor of my own time. And yet . . . in no course of life have I been ever more closely pressed by business than in the present . . . leaving little time for indulgence in my greatest of all amusements, reading. Doctor Franklin used to say that when he was young, and had time to read, he had not books; and now when he had become old and had books, he had no time.[29]

After discussing politics with another friend, Jefferson wrote, "My delight is now in the passive occupation of reading; and it is with great reluctance I permit my mind ever to encounter subjects of difficult investigation."[30] Jefferson similarly wrote to his friend and former secretary William Short of the consolation reading the classics brought, "My business is to beguile the wearisomeness of declining life, as I endeavor to do, by the delights of classical reading."[31] On another occasion Jefferson wrote in a depressed mood of the importance of classical education because reading the classics comforted those about to die:

> When the decays of age have enfeebled the useful energies of the mind, the classic pages fill up the vacuum of *ennui*,

and become sweet composers to that rest of the grave into which we are all sooner or later to descend.[32]

A more cheerful picture of Jefferson's enjoyment of reading in his retirement was given by Randall in the recollections of one of Jefferson's younger granddaughters:

> On winter evenings, when it grew too dark to read, in the half hour that passed before candles came in, as we all sat around the fire, he taught us several childish games and would play them with us. . . . When the candles were brought, all was quiet immediately, for he took up his book to read, and we would not speak out of a whisper lest we should disturb him, and generally we followed his example and took a book—and I have seen him raise his eyes from his own book and look round on the little circle of readers, and smile and make some remark to mamma about it.[33]

There is no question but that reading was a source of great pleasure to Jefferson all during his life. He highly valued his books and constantly made good use of them.

Jefferson's Interest in Book Collecting. Because of his love of reading and his urge to gather and arrange information, Jefferson was concerned all of his adult life with collecting books in private libraries for the use of himself and his friends. Stimulated by his most influential college teachers Dr. William Small and George Wythe[34] and by the expanding horizons of the Enlightenment, Jefferson's intellectual curiosity extended to all sorts of fields, from agriculture, medicine, and science to politics, economics, and religion. Lehmann observes:

> Jefferson's approach to understanding the entirety of the intelligible world, natural and human . . . was encyclopedic, in the original meaning of the word; that is, it aimed at an all-inclusive knowledge of facts related to each other.[35]

Evidence of Jefferson's encyclopedic interest is seen in the fact that one of the first of his major book purchases was the *Encyclo-*

pédie from an Alexandrian agent in exchange for "tobacco notes."[36]

Jefferson was not unique in his wide-ranging quest for knowledge, for this intellectual interest was widespread in the eighteenth century. Isaac Newton, John Locke, Francis Bacon, and Voltaire are but some of many men of this period who used their means to collect books and their leisure for study. It was a time that emphasized man's reason, and man's knowledge had not yet grown beyond the capacity of a diligent student to comprehend nor beyond the compass of one man's library to hold. Thomas Jefferson holds a unique position in the eighteenth-century world of being not only a leader of intellectual thought but also a leader who embodied Enlightenment thought in historical action. Jefferson's national and world leadership depended upon his wide reading and thorough knowledge of government, history, and the thought of the intellectual leaders of his time.

If Jefferson was not unique in his thirst for knowledge and his zeal in collecting books, he certainly was exceptional among his friends of the Virginian aristocracy. Probably influenced by Small and Wythe, he had early gathered a modest library based on his college texts, law books, and the commonplace notebooks he had copied from borrowed books he studied. When the home at Shadwell where Jefferson lived with his mother burned, it was the loss of his books, valued at "£200 sterling," that most disturbed Jefferson. He wrote to his college friend John Page, "Would to God it had been the money, *then* had it never cost me a sigh!"[37]

Jefferson quickly set about building a new private library, for his correspondence contains many references to purchasing books.[38] An early letter to John Randolph, for example, requested the opportunity to purchase books from Randolph's library, particularly on "parliamentary learning," since Randolph was "going to the land of literature and books," Great Britain, where he might "replace them there in better editions."[39] Jefferson was also interested in the library of "Colonel Richard Bland one of our delegates in Congress, a great antiquarian, and possessed of many valuable public papers," and purchased his library when he died in 1776.[40] Somewhat later Jefferson wrote to James Madison from Annapolis of "hunting out and buying books" for his own collection and offered to order them for Madison also.[41]

For Jefferson, one of the most enjoyable aspects of being sent abroad to represent the United States was the opportunity to buy books from European booksellers who provided a wider selection at better prices than was obtainable then in the United States. Jefferson's correspondence while abroad contains many references to buying books from London booksellers. In 1785 John Stockdale answered a query from Jefferson stating that he would obtain requested books from Scotland and would send "such publications as are valuable by every opportunity." Jefferson could settle his account "once or twice a Year . . . in London when convenient."[42] In another letter to Stockdale, Jefferson placed an order for a group of books that included Homer's *Iliad* and *Odyssey*, a Greek lexicon, some works of American history, Priestley's "Biographical Chart," and the works of Shakespeare to be sent from London to Paris by stage coach.[43] In a letter to a friend in London, Jefferson requested his friend to purchase books for him at "Stockdale" and "Lackington" bookstores.[44]

In addition, since he was proficient in reading French, Jefferson enjoyed himself browsing through the bookstores in Paris. He recalled happily years later:

> While residing in Paris, I devoted every afternoon I was disengaged for a summer or two, in examining all the principal bookstores, turning over every book with my own hand, and putting by everything which related to America, and indeed whatever was rare and valuable in every science.[45]

Jefferson further took advantage of his travels while in Europe and of his contacts with friends in other countries to collect books from other sources:

> Besides this, I had standing orders during the whole time I was in Europe, on its principal book-marts, particularly Amsterdam, Frankfort, Madrid, and London, for such works relating to America as could not be found in Paris.[46]

[26]

Jefferson's correspondence documents his book collecting. In 1785 William Carmichael wrote Jefferson of purchasing part of the "Library of a Spanish Gentleman" for him which included works on the Spanish settlements in America.[47] There are also orders to the book seller Van Damme in Amsterdam for books including Greek and Latin classics, a Greek-Latin dictionary, a Gallic dictionary, and a Dutch-English dictionary, indicating that Jefferson was keeping up with his studies.[48]

Jefferson could not forbear sharing his opportunities for book bargains with his friends. Madison gladly accepted Jefferson's offer to purchase "either old and curious or new and useful" works, especially bargains in law books, history, and Greek and Roman authors.[49] Jefferson sent Madison a three-page list of works he was endeavoring to obtain.[50] Eventually he shipped "three trunks and a box of books" to Madison and Edmund Randolph by ship.[51] A year later, Jefferson sent three more boxes of books from France, he wrote Madison, "one marked I. M. for yourself, one marked B. F. for Doctor Franklin, and one marked W. H. for William Hay."[52] The following year Jefferson executed a book commission for another friend, for he wrote Alexander Donald, "The box of books I had taken the liberty to address to you is but just gone from Havre for New York."[53]

Much of the reason for Jefferson's enthusiastic collecting of books while in Europe was not just the wider choice and the lower prices for standard works found there but the broader cultural and intellectual choices. Jefferson, in reporting his impressions of France to friends back home, was critical of the poverty and ignorance of the people and the immorality of the upper classes, but he admired their manners, culture, and devotion to the arts and literature.

> In science, the mass of the people are two centuries behind ours; their literati, half a dozen years before us. Books, really good, acquire just reputation in that time, and so become known to us, and communicate to us all their advances in knowledge.[54]

After returning from France to America, Jefferson continued his interest in sending books to his friends and family. His family letters, for example, include mention of sending books to his married daughter Martha, along with household furniture, from Philadelphia, where Jefferson was serving in Washington's cabinet. He also sent books on the history of the Spanish settlement in Florida "to be deposited in my library."[55] In 1803 he sent a "French Grammar" to his grandson so that "I shall be able to ask you, 'Parlez vous Francais, monsieur?' "[56] He was no doubt pleased to receive a prompt reply:

> We have been expecting the measles but have escaped it as yet. Virginia has learnt to speak very well. Ellen is learning french. Cornelia sends her love to you. I would be very much obliged to you if you would bring me a book of geography. Adieu Dear GrandPapa.[57]

It is clear that Jefferson was consulted by his friends not only for advice on where to buy books but also on what books to buy. An example is the latitude Madison allowed Jefferson in purchasing books for him in France, and the way Madison's order for some classic works, historical works, and "new or curious" works expanded into a three-page list.[58] It is noteworthy that Jefferson could discuss and explain each work that Madison might not know.[59]

Another example of Jefferson's friends consulting him for advice in selecting books occurred when his brother-in-law Robert Skipwith asked him to "form a catalogue of books amounting to about thirty pounds sterling." Jefferson could not restrain himself to such a small library and responded by drawing up what seemed to him the minimum adequate selection of the most important works of fiction, literature, poetry, politics and trade, religion, law, ancient history, modern history, and natural history and philosophy. Despite the strictest economy of editions and binding (Jefferson warned that elegant, gilt bindings would cost fifty percent more) the cost came to many times thirty pounds and extended to over 150 titles. Jefferson suggested Skipwith might buy the volumes he liked best the first year and "complete the whole . . . hereafter as shall be convenient." Even better, Jefferson suggested, Skipwith and his wife, "our dear Tibby," could move to the family home near Monticello, "the new Rowanty, from which you may reach

your hand to a library formed on a more extensive plan. . . .
There we should talk over the lessons of the day."[60]

The Importance of Books in Education. For Jefferson, collecting
books and forming libraries was always a means to an end. The
art of beautiful bookbinding and collecting first editions had
little appeal for him. Plain, durable bindings of useful works
packed with notes and comments were what Jefferson sought,
and when he had duplicate titles of the same work it was for
the purpose of comparison and study. Commenting on Jefferson's interest in collecting books only as "useful tools," William
Peden concludes from his study of Jefferson's book collecting:

> It cannot be said that he possessed the instincts of the
> bibliophile. He had no interest in rare books or early edi-
> tions as such . . .
> He had an ardent desire to encourage the art of printing
> in the United States, but not because it was an art. His
> interest in printing was largely a utilitarian one.[61]

Books and libraries were, in Jefferson's understanding, important tools for expanding the mind of man, and as essential
for the lawyer and scholar as an ax for the woodsman and a
plow for the farmer. He was generous in sharing both his
knowledge of books and the facilities of his library with friends
seeking advice.

Jefferson's influence upon the reading and education of his
younger friend and colleague James Madison has been noted
by scholars, and their close collaboration in the struggles for
freedom, religious liberty, and the extension of American democracy remarked.[62] James Monroe was another young man whose
education and career were aided by Jefferson. "The historically
important three-cornered friendship of Jefferson, Madison, and
Monroe was conceived and deliberately arranged by Jefferson's
own prudent hand," Koch comments,[63] a friendship that resulted
in the longest administration of one point of view in American
political history. Jefferson not only introduced Monroe to
Madison but also to Benjamin Franklin, John Adams, and John
Jay,[64] and advised him on books of law to study and books of
science that he could obtain when he traveled to Paris. Jeffer-

son advised Monroe to "attend Westminster hall a term or two."[65] Monroe wrote of his gratitude for Jefferson's help during the troubled time of his life when he was deciding what work to pursue after "a variety of disappointments."

> In this situation you became acquainted with me and undertook the direction of my studies and believe me I feel that whatever I am at present in the opinion of others or whatever I may be in future has greatly arose [sic] from your friendship.[66]

As early as 1769 Jefferson wrote to a friend explaining that he was unable "to undertake the superintendance of your son in his studies" of law because he was in the process of building his home at Monticello and had no room to lodge the young man. Instead he "laid down a plan of study" the youth could follow on his own, rather than wasting his time as an apprentice working for the "emolument" of an older lawyer. It would be necessary, however, to purchase the books which Jefferson recommended, "for a lawyer without books would be like a workman without tools." Jefferson suggested the £100 cost would be money well spent as providing for the son's future.[67]

Jefferson was even more closely involved in supervising the education of his children and near relatives and in guiding their reading. Such supervision was customary in colonial Virginia, but Jefferson clearly gave more guidance that was usual because of his interest in books and education. He wrote encouraging letters to his daughters to study diligently while in the convent school in France,[68] and took even more interest in the more challenging education of his male relatives. He wrote to his nephew Peter Carr urging him to study harder and make up for "lost time," and recommended studies in classical reading, history, and the works of Milton, Pope, and Ossian. He enclosed a list of books for Carr to purchase, including "a clever little encyclopédie" by Beaumart which "costs about 48f."[69] In a later letter, Jefferson showed his concern for Carr's studies by giving him good advice on how to use his own reason in studying morality and religion and enclosed a list of a few of the most important books which he advised Carr to study in

history, poetry, science, morality, and religion.   All presented
the Enlightenment point of view.[70]

Years later, Jefferson was equally concerned with the education of his grandson Francis Wayles Eppes. Because of lack of
money until the sale of crops at home, young Eppes had to leave
college before the lectures in some of his courses were completed.
He wrote to Jefferson outlining his plans to finish studying the
courses on his own.[71] Jefferson replied agreeing that his grandson could well study on his own and outlined a plan to study
law for four or five hours a day, relieved by further reading in
science, belles lettres, history and ethics.   Jefferson drew up a
list of books and offered to "procure" them from "the sum I have
to pay your father."[72]

That Jefferson took pleasure both from his own reading and
from sharing his reading with others is made plain in an account he wrote of his retirement "where, in the bosom of my
family, and surrounded by my books, I enjoy . . . repose."

> A part of my occupation, and by no means the least pleasing,
> is the direction of the studies of such young men as ask it.
> They place themselves in the neighboring village, and have
> the use of my library and counsel, and make a part of my
> society.[73]

The sharing of the use of his library and his wide knowledge
of books and information was clearly very important to Jefferson. He generously expended his time and effort on close friends
and promising protégés, family and relatives, and even comparative strangers who came to him for help.

Jefferson's broad library interest is seen in the fact that over
the years he developed well-considered ideas about courses of
reading and methods of study for various subjects. In letters to
a law student and to Dr. Thomas Cooper who was teaching law,
Jefferson outlined the branches of English law to study in proper
order and the definitive works to be mastered in each branch.[74]
He wrote a comprehensive essay on the importance of studying
Greek and Latin classics for various professions to a classical
scholar.[75] To a university professor, Jefferson wrote a learned
discussion of the most important works to read in both ancient

history and English and American history, stating, "In all cases I prefer original authors to compilers."[76] Jefferson's reading interests and subject knowledge were indeed encyclopedic.

Besides directing the reading and education of young lawyers, statesmen, and male relatives, Jefferson took considerable interest in the education of his daughters, although he clearly regarded the education of young women as of lesser importance and a lesser challenge, for he wrote to a fellow Virginian aristocrat:

> A plan of female education has never been a subject of systematic contemplation with me. It has occupied my attention so far only as the education of my own daughters occasionally required.[77]

Since education must be tailored to the purposes and needs of the student, Jefferson's recommended courses of study for young women of his time were much different from those he urged upon young men. The solid classics, extensive readings in history and science, and heavy study of law were completely absent. Instead he suggested the "accomplishments" for "circles of festivity" such as "dancing, drawing, and music" which would give the young woman social graces. French language study was recommended to enhance culture, as was a study of moral literature, although Jefferson deplored the "inordinate passion prevalent for novels" and "too much poetry" which made ordinary living and study seem dull and uninteresting by contrast. Jefferson praised but passed lightly over "household economy, in which the mothers of our country are generally skilled, and generally careful to instruct their daughters. We all know its value."[78]

Jefferson's purpose was to prepare his daughters for the social life, to be pleasant companions and aids for their husbands as well as good homemakers, and to have the basic education necessary to supervise the primary education of the children on the plantation.

> I thought it essential to give them a solid education, which might enable them, when become mothers, to educate their own daughters, and even to direct the course for sons, should their fathers be lost, or incapable, or inattentive.[79]

THOMAS JEFFERSON, LIBRARIAN

Although the courses of study might be lighter for girls, Jefferson urged the same diligence. In an early letter to "my dear Patsy" after her mother had died, Jefferson wrote of "the tutors I have provided for you" and "the situation I have placed you in" for your improvement (it was with the family of a Philadelphia friend, Mrs. Thomas Hopkinson).[80] He urged upon his daughter a busy day of study:

> With respect to the distribution of your time the following is what I should approve: from 8 to 10 o'clock practise [sic] music, from 10 to 1 dance one day and draw another, from 1 to 2 draw on the day you dance, and write a letter the next day, from 3 to 4 read French, from 4 to 5 exercise yourself in music, from 5 till bedtime read English, write, etc.[81]

Jefferson's attitude towards "female education" may seem to reflect male chauvinism to modern liberated women, but it probably did no more than represent the realistic situation confronting women in his time. That Jefferson admired and respected the part his daughter played in the family can be seen in the deference he paid to her ability and judgment in the same letter to Burwell:

> My surviving daughter . . . , the mother of many daughters as well as sons, has made their education the object of her life, and being a better judge of the practical part than myself, it is with her aid . . . that I shall subjoin a catalogue of the books for such a course of reading as we have practiced.[82]

The list of recommended reading has unfortunately been lost, but again the practice shows Jefferson's practical interest in the use of books.

That Jefferson was well aware of the importance of books and libraries for the proper education of men and women and devoted a good deal of his time, wealth, and effort to this purpose is well documented, then, by his writings. He also was one of the foremost leaders of his generation who saw the importance of reading and education for the happiness and advancement of human welfare. Jefferson's concern for improved education has been well documented and studied by scholars.[83] After independence was achieved, one of the earliest reforms he proposed for the new American democracy in Virginia was a comprehensive program of public education.[84] As Jefferson recalled in his *Autobiography*:

> I accordingly prepared three bills for the Revisal, proposing three distinct grades of education, reaching all classes. 1. Elementary schools for all children generally, rich and poor. 2. Colleges for a middle degree of instruction, calculated for the common purposes of life, and such as would be desirable for all who were in easy circumstances. And 3d. an ultimate grade for teaching the sciences generally, and in their highest degree.[85]

One of the achievements of Jefferson's retirement was the fulfillment of this last goal, a university of higher education, in the establishment of the University of Virginia.[86] An important part of all his aims for education was the establishment of libraries as part of the schools.[87]

Even more important than Jefferson's concern for reading and education are the purposes he saw such reading fulfilling. Jefferson was one of the first of Enlightenment proponents of the right of men to rule themselves to see that only reasonable, educated men could be successful in the experiment of democratic self-rule. While in France observing the ignorance and exploitation of the common people there, Jefferson wrote to his law mentor George Wythe:

> Preach, my dear Sir, a crusade against ignorance; establish and improve the law for educating the common people. . . . The tax which will be paid for this purpose, is not more than the thousandth part of what will be paid to kings, priests and nobles, who will rise up among us if we leave the people in ignorance.[88]

Many years later, Jefferson wrote to his old friend of the American and French Revolutions, Lafayette, "Ignorance and bigotry, like other insanities, are incapable of self-government."[89] To another French friend of the Enlightenment, Jefferson wrote:

[34]

Enlighten the people generally and tyranny and oppressions
of body and mind will vanish like evil spirits at the dawn
of day. Although I do not, with some enthusiasts, believe
that the human condition will ever advance to such a state
of perfection as that there shall no longer be pain or vice
in the world, yet I believe it susceptible of much improvement . . . and that the diffusion of knowledge among
the people is the instrument by which it is to be effected.[90]

Besides progress in government, Jefferson looked to free education and open investigation to bring progress in society, particularly from "the free range of mind" and "unequalled order
of science . . . encouraged" at the new University of Virginia.

The effect of this institution on the future fame, fortune
and prosperity of our country, can as yet be seen but at a
distance. But an hundred well-educated youths, which it
will turn out annually, and ere long, will fill all its offices
with men of superior qualifications.[91]

Besides these advantages to society, Jefferson looked to reading
and education to make for a more able citizen, better able to
conduct his own private affairs, "to improve, by reading, his
morals and faculties, . . . to understand his duties . . . , to
know his rights, . . . to form statesmen, legislators and judges,
. . . to develop the reasoning faculties of our youth, [and] to
enlighten them."[92]

Jefferson thus saw the purpose of education as being both
private and social. As a guide for his own education of young
men who came to him for the direction of their reading in
his library, Jefferson concluded:

In advising the course of their reading, I endeavor to keep
their attention fixed on the main objects of all science, the
freedom and happiness of man. So that coming to bear a
share in the councils and government of their country, they
will keep ever in view the sole objects of all legitimate government.[93]

For Jefferson, above and beyond the personal and social purposes of reading and education was the great purpose of God for enlightening mankind. "The cultivation of science . . . [and our] minds is a religious duty to the Author of our being," he wrote.[94] Jefferson lived by this creed of study and education.

The Importance of Public Libraries. Because of his belief in the importance of an educated citizenry in a republic and the religious duty of men to pursue enlightenment and self-development, Jefferson was far ahead of his time in proposing the establishment of public libraries, as some Jeffersonian scholars have briefly noted.[95] As part of his comprehensive plan for public education which proposed the establishment of primary schools, high schools, and a university, Jefferson drew a Bill for Establishing a Public Library[96] which, he explained, "proposed . . . to begin a public library and gallery, by laying out a certain sum annually in books, paintings, and statues."[97] As Boyd notes, Jefferson was not planning a circulation library similar to Benjamin Franklin's Library Company of Philadelphia, with which Jefferson must have become acquainted on his earlier trips to Philadelphia.[98] Nor did he have in mind anything comparable to a modern public library, since the regulations he proposed made it unlawful for "any . . . persons to remove any book or map out of the said library."[99] Jefferson was evidently proposing a reference reserve library, free for any interested person to use but probably intended as a particular aid for the members of the Virginian legislature, since it was to be located in Richmond.

Jefferson also had a hand in trying to establish a similar reference library for the use of members of the United States Congress. His library-minded friend Colonel Bland and James Madison were members of the actual committee, but there is evidence Jefferson had a hand in preparing the list of recommended books for the proposed congressional library. The committee's recommended book list was similar to the "1783 Catalogue" of books which Jefferson was preparing as a guide for his book purchases when he arrived in France, and he and Madison roomed in the same house in Philadelphia during these months.[100]

On another occasion, Jefferson recorded his support of public libraries "for the promotion of knowledge among my country-men" and "to instruct . . . the people [who] are the only safe guardians of their own rights . . . [so that] they would never . . . be . . . deceived." Jefferson added:

> I have often thought that nothing would do more extensive good at small expense than the establishment of a small circulating library in every county, to consist of a few well-chosen books, to be lent to the people of the country, under such regulations as would secure their safe return in due time.[101]

Because of his interest in promoting education, Jefferson gave a high priority to encouraging the collecting of books and the establishment and use of libraries, both private and public.

Jefferson's Personal Libraries

Even more than his concern with public libraries or with helping his friends to form personal libraries, most of his biographers have commented on Jefferson's interest in forming his own personal library. Most have noted how he began as a student to create a library from his text books, law books, commonplace books, and favorite authors, and noted that he had to start over after fire destroyed his home at Shadwell.[102] Lehmann comments on Jefferson's library interest:

> His efforts to acquire the books he needed to satisfy his ever expanding thirst for knowledge in general . . . re-sulted in his assembling libraries, one after another, in spite of the misfortunes which he encountered.[103]

After the loss of Jefferson's first library "he began to build up the amazing library which was his pride until he sold it to Congress in 1815," Lehmann notes, [104] and it is this library to which most of Jefferson's writings and most of the comments by Jeffersonian scholars refer. Within three years after losing his first library, Jefferson had replaced his books so that his library was larger than before.[105] He recorded 1,256 volumes in his library in his account book for 1773.[106] In his *Diary* under the date August 4, 1773, Jefferson recorded:

My library.

In the mahogany book case with glass doors .... 510 vols.
Walnut book case in N. W. corner of room .... 180 vols.
Walnut book case in N. E. corner of room .... 224 vols.
Shelves in N. W. corner of room .... 157 vols.
Shelves in N. E. corner of room .... 131 vols.
Lent out .... 42 vols.
Lying about .... 10 vols.
Note this does not include vols. of Music, nor my books
in Williamsburgh.[107]

We may note, in passing, Jefferson's willingness to act as a lending librarian for his friends but notice how uncharacteristic it
was to his librarian's orderly ways to have ten volumes "lying
about." Probably they were in use.

Over the years Jefferson took every opportunity to add to his
library, first from the booksellers in Williamsburg, then Annapolis and Philadelphia, and later in London, Paris and Amsterdam.[108]   Before sailing for France, Jefferson had leisure to
complete the cataloging of his library to guide himself in the
book purchases he planned to make abroad.[109]   By that time,
1783, his library had grown to 2,640 volumes and Jefferson had
arranged his library by subject matter based on Lord Bacon's
"table of sciences,"[110] instead of by bookcases as in his first
inventory.

By the time of his retirement, Jefferson's library had more than
tripled, for in a letter to Dr. Thomas Cooper about his hopes
for establishing a university in Virginia, Jefferson described his
own library in these words:

> This consists of about seven or eight thousand volumes, the
> best chosen collection of its size probably in America, and
> containing a great mass of what is most rare and valuable,
> and especially of what relates to America.[111]

During that same year of 1814, in a letter in which Jefferson
proposed to sell his library to Congress "at their own price"
to replace the library destroyed during the War of 1812, Jefferson
further described his library:

You know my collection, its condition and extent. I have been fifty years making it, and have spared no pains, opportunity or expense, to make it what it is. . . . So that the collection, which I suppose is of between nine and ten thousand volumes, while it includes what is chiefly valuable in science and literature generally, extends more particularly to whatever belongs to the American statesman. . . . Nearly the whole are well bound, abundance of them elegantly, and of the choicest editions existing.[112]

Occasional references to Jefferson's library at Monticello occur in the writings of those that saw it. Chastellux mentions the library as being a prominent part of the Monticello he saw in 1782:

This house, of which Mr. Jefferson was the architect, and often one of the workmen, is rather elegant; . . . it consists of one large square pavilion, the entrance of which is by two porticos ornamented with pillars. The ground floor consists chiefly of a very large lofty saloon, which is to be decorated entirely in the antique style: above it is a library of the same form.[113]

In 1815 George Ticknor, who became a trusted agent for obtaining books for Jefferson in his later years, visited Monticello. He wrote of traveling up a "steep, savage hill" by a "pensive and slow" winding road to the "artificial lawn" and "brick . . . house . . . built, I suppose, in the French style." Then Ticknor described the library:

On Sunday morning, after breakfast, Mr. Jefferson asked me into his library, and there I spent the forenoon of that day as I had that of yesterday. This collection of books, now so much talked about, consists of about seven thousand volumes, contained in a suite of fine rooms, and is arranged in the cataloge, and on the shelves, according to the divisions and subdivisions of human learning by Lord Bacon.[114]

Members of Jefferson's family recalled the prominent part his library played in his daily life at Monticello. A grandson remembered Jefferson spending much time in "his own apartments, which consisted of a bed-chamber and library opening into each other, . . . occupied in reading, writing, looking over papers, etc."[115] The slave Isaac Jefferson also remembered Jefferson working in his library "till bell ring for dinner." He recalled:

> When writing he had a copyin machine: while he was a-writin he wouldn't suffer nobody to come in his room: had a dumb-waiter: when he wanted anything he had nothin to do but turn a crank and the dumb-waiter would bring him water or fruit on a plate or anything he wanted.[116]

Jefferson used the library rooms for more than reading and writing; he also used them for planning architecture and building projects at the plantation. Isaac remembered Jefferson advising and working with him on such projects: ·

> My Old Master was as neat a hand as ever you see to make keys and locks and small chains, iron and brass; he kept all kind of blacksmith and carpenter tools in a great case with shelves to it in his library, an upstairs room. Isaac went up thar constant: been up thar a thousand times.[117]

Most likely the book cases and shelves of his library, as well as the arrangement of the books, were the handiwork of Jefferson and his plantation workmen.[118] His plans for bookshelves and an ingenious folding ladder to reach the higher shelves have been preserved.[119] Jefferson himself described the bookcases and their construction when he was making plans for shipping the library to Washington:

> The books stand at present in pine cases with backs and shelves without fronts. The cases are generally of three tier, one upon another, about nine feet high in the whole . . .
> . . . The books should go in their cases, every one its station, so that the cases on their arrival need only be set up on end, and they will be arranged exactly as they stand in the catalogue. I will have the fronts closed with boards for the journey, which being taken off on their arrival at Washington, sash doors may be made there at little expense.

But the books will require careful . . . packing, to prevent
their being rubbed in so long and rough a journey by . . .
waggons.[120]

During his long residence at Monticello Jefferson located
his fine library in two places in his home. He first located his
library in the room on the second floor described by Chastellux
and Isaac Jefferson where the mahogany and walnut bookcases
inventoried by Jefferson were located. In 1796, however, Jefferson got the urge to rebuild Monticello and erected a domed
roof over the center portion of his mansion. The library was
moved to the ground floor pavilion, facing south and "extending
through the depth of the house."[121] It was this second library
apartment, adjoining Jefferson's bedroom, which Ticknor saw
and which was described by Jefferson's grandchildren.[122]

The library collection Jefferson sold to Congress, which became
the real beginning of the Library of Congress, was noteworthy
not only for its wide and careful selection of important works
but also for its preservation of historic papers, "rare colonial
newspaper files and precious manuscripts in Virginia history,
. . . such as the records of the Virginia Company of London,
. . . many acquired by legacy [and] purchase from Virginia
estates."[123] Although Jefferson chose his books for their
content and ease of handling rather than their elegance of binding, he spared no expense, as Koch notes:

Elegant bindings done by his own American binders testi-
fied to his incurably cultivated tastes. Jefferson could
correctly claim that his extensive collection was unsur-
passed in its holdings on America, and that it was at the same
time broader and more general in scope than any other
library in the country.[124]

After Jefferson sold his library to Congress he could not
resist buying more books with part of the proceeds and so began
his third library, the one for his old age "running eventually
to about a thousand volumes."[125] Jefferson took advantage
of his friendship with "Mr. Ticknor . . . the best bibliograph
I have met" who was going abroad to study, for "reprocuring
some part of the literary treasures which I have ceded to Congress

[41]

to replace the devastations of British Vandalism at Washington."[126] As Koch comments:

> No sooner had the crates departed [containing the books of his library] than the habit of fifty years reasserted itself. A man wedded to books is apparently as hard to cope with as a man wedded to the bottle. He began to order again, drawing to the Monticello mountain top for his twilight years the great classical writers and moralists whom he had always revered; the political philosophers; the educators with new theories; the liberal religionists; the historians; books on agriculture—in short, the multitudinous subjects of interest to a powerful intellect that drew no harsh lines in the seamless web of knowledge.[127]

Jefferson himself said, "I cannot live without books: but fewer will suffice where amusement, and not use, is the only future object."[128] Jefferson's idea of amusement was a studious one, for his third library consisted of many reference works as well as favorite classical and mathematical tomes.[129] Tracing the growth of this last library which Jefferson began when he was seventy-two and developed over the last ten years of his life into "a well chosen library of approximately a thousand individual items,"[130] Peden concluded:

> Almost until the time of his death Thomas Jefferson continued to add to his library. . . . The next to the last item in his account book, dated June 13, 1826, just a little over a fortnight before his death . . . is as follows: "Dr. Emmit for a book."[131]

Jefferson willed his last collection of books to the University of Virginia and any duplicates to "my two grandsons-in-law,"[132] but the books actually were sold at auction on his death to meet expenses of the estate and were dispersed.[133]

Jefferson early formed the habit of having a traveling library to keep with him when away from home. In the early inventory of his books at Monticello he mentioned "other books" which he kept at Williamsburg.[134] While at Washington, Jefferson made what he called his "petit-format library" to use there, and

when he retired he transferred it to his summer home, Poplar
Forest. Randall, using the recollections of Jefferson's grandchildren, who used to accompany him on his extended visits
to Poplar Forest, described the library as consisting of upwards
of one hundred favorite works

> contained in four cases, each of which was perhaps between
> three and four feet in width and height. The books, to
> economize space, were generally of the smallest sized edi-
> tions published.[135]

Wherever he went throughout his long life Jefferson was
continually engaged in collecting books and creating libraries.
It may be fairly agreed that he was right when he wrote, "Books
are indeed with me a necessary of life."[136]

Jefferson and the University of Virginia Library

Although it was not formed for his own personal use, the
library of the University of Virginia is usually mentioned in
connection with Jefferson's own libraries because he took such
an important part in its formation. Jefferson personally selected
the books for the library to support the courses and curriculum,
which he also drew up for the university.[137] He spent most of
his working hours for several months, he wrote Madison, selecting the books to purchase from his own "collection of excellent
catalogues, . . . knowing no one capable, to whom we could
refer the task. It has been laborious far beyond my expectation."
He did refer to Madison for a list of books on "divinity."[138] As
Elizabeth Cometti has described, he ordered the books from
distant booksellers and arranged for a Bostonian to set up a
college bookstore to sell textbooks. Although by now old and
in poor health, he helped with the unpacking, cataloging, and
arranging of some of the books when they arrived.[139] Despite
pressure to get the university operating as soon as some of the
classrooms and dormitories were completed, Jefferson insisted
it was necessary to complete the building housing the library
before opening the university for students.[140] Jefferson, moreover, wrote the "library regulations" which provided for full
use of the library by the faculty at all times, for lending books

to the students "for reading only" and not as a substitute for their own textbooks, provided fines for failing to care for or to return any book, and provided for a librarian to keep records of books lent out and to supervise reading in the library on certain hours and certain days of the week.[141]

This attention to detail was typical of Jefferson's concern for the university. The establishment of the university was more than "a Hobby . . . against this tedium vitae ['weariness of life']," as Jefferson himself called it,[142] or "a noble employment in your old Age," as John Adams called it,[143] but was the crowning achievement of Jefferson's life, which he wished recorded on his tombstone.[144] In 1778 Jefferson had proposed such a university as part of a comprehensive program of public education, but it was not until 1819, when Jefferson was seventy-five years old, that the act establishing the university was passed. Jefferson's plan for public schools on the elementary levels was not fulfilled by Virginia until the 1870s, long after he was dead. For the last seven years of his life Jefferson worked as chairman or rector of the board of visitors to bring his dream of an enlightened institution of higher learning in the South into reality.[145] He wrote the report setting the aims, curriculum, philosophy, and academic organization for the university.[146] He developed the plan for "an academic village" for the campus with a separate building for each department "arranged around an open square of grass and trees" instead "of making one large and expensive building . . . a common den of noise, of filth and of fetid air"[147] which influenced the future development of American universities. He made the plans for the university buildings and supervised their construction.[148] He wrote Adams of riding horseback four miles to the university, although he could "walk but little," to "direct it's architecture. It's plan is unique, and it is becoming an object of curiosity for the traveller."[149]

Honeywell sums up Jefferson's influence upon the University of Virginia in this manner:

> Scarcely an institution exists which can so aptly be described in the words of Emerson as "the lengthened shadow of one man." He bought the site for the university and surveyed

it. He planned the buildings and superintended their construction. He wrung funds from a niggardly legislature while he sought even the smallest economy in the cost of bricks. The course of study, the plan of organization, the rules for admission, graduation, and government—all were his work. He set standards of democracy for the faculty and of manly self-reliance for the students. Nearly every detail of material construction, or organization, or of method was his. He was more than a founder. He was Father of the University of Virginia.[150]

At last he saw it open and functioning, and within a year he was dead.

It is a tribute to Jefferson's dedication to the importance of books and libraries in the work of education that he refused to yield to the temptation that many educators under similar pressures have yielded to, of slighting the library. He not only insisted upon providing the library building but also insisted upon providing the 6,860 carefully chosen volumes, costing $24,076, which he considered the essential nucleus for the university library.[151]. Even after the books had been ordered and began to arrive at the university, Jefferson's troubles were not over. The first books to arrive seem to have been arranged in a temporary room of the first pavilion erected,[152] since the planned central room for the library was slow in being finished, much to Jefferson's annoyance. He wrote to Madison:

> I rode to the University and desired Mr. Brockenbrough to . . . stop everything which could be done without, and to emply all his force and funds in finishing the circular room for the books, and the anatomical theatre. These cannot be done without. . . . In the meantime, there have arrived for us in different ports of the United States, ten boxes of books from Paris, seven from London, and from Germany I know not how many; in all, perhaps, about twenty-five boxes. Not one of these can be opened until the bookroom is completely finished, and all the shelves ready to receive their charge directly from the boxes as they shall be opened. This cannot be till May.[153]

[45]

The library room, unfortunately, was not finished by May or even by the summer of 1826 when Jefferson died, so that he never did see the books he had so carefully selected arranged in his fine "circular room." His plans were realized by that fall, however, for one of the new students, Edgar Allan Poe, wrote home, "They have nearly finished the Rotunda—the pillars of the Portico are completed and it greatly improves the appearance of the whole. The books are removed into the library, and we have a very fine collection."[154] Jefferson was right to insist that books were as necessary for his young men as for himself.

Jefferson and the Library of Congress

From the earliest days, Thomas Jefferson was closely associated with establishing a library for the use of the Congress. While the Congress met in New York City and then in Philadelphia, little need was felt for a library of its own since its members had access to the New York State Society Library, and in Philadelphia they had free use of the facilities of the Library Company of that city. During this period the library for members of Congress consisted of only a few shelves of reference works, according to Gene Gurney:

> Congress . . . had found it necessary to acquire a few standard reference works—Blackstone's *Commentaries*, Vattel's *Law of Nature and Nations*, Hume's *History of England*, Morse's *American Geography*—in all some 50 titles, plus subscriptions to a few periodicals.[155]

It was a different story, however, when Congress moved to the new, raw city of Washington, D.C. No libraries were then in existence there so Congress appointed a library committee to see about establishing a library for Congress. Although Jefferson was not then a member of the Congress nor of the library committee—he was awaiting passage to France as American minister—he was in close contact with James Madison and Colonel Bland who were, and the catalogue of books which Jefferson was preparing for his own library and book purchases was used by Madison for the booklist recommended to Congress.[156] Madison's condensed list from Jefferson's 1783

Catalogue of Books proved more than Congress was willing to adopt.[157] It was not until 1800 that Congress appropriated the sum of $5,000 "for the purchase of such books as may be necessary for the use of Congress at the said city of Washington, and for fitting up a suitable apartment for containing them." Eventually 740 volumes were sent from London in "eleven hair trunks."[158]

In 1802, Thomas Jefferson, as President of the United States, chose an old friend John James Beckley as the first librarian of Congress. Beckley was really clerk of the House of Representatives and was paid $2.00 a day extra for the days he issued books. Jefferson also was active in advising on the works to be chosen for the library, emphasizing histories, books on law of nature and nations, encyclopedias, dictionaries in various languages, and reference works on general law subjects.[159]

Over the years the congressional library slowly grew until by 1814, it had accumulated 3,000 volumes. It was unfortunate that they were housed in a small committee room in the new capitol building because in 1814 British soldiers found them good kindling to use in burning the Capitol when they captured Washington in the War of 1812. A public outcry over this burning of books arose in both the United States and Great Britain and the need was felt to replace the Library of Congress.[160] When Thomas Jefferson, retired from the presidency and living at Monticello, heard of the "British Vandalism,"[161] he wrote to Samuel Harrison Smith, member of the library committee, offering to sell his own library at cost as a legacy to Congress. He wrote:

> You know my collection, its condition and extent. . . .
> It is long since I have been sensible it ought not to continue private property, and had provided that, at my death, Congress should have the refusal of it, at their own price. But the loss they have incurred makes the present the proper moment for this accommodation without regard to the small remnant of time and the barren use of my enjoyment.[162]

At the same time Jefferson wrote to Madison, who was president of the United States, of his reasons for offering his library to Congress:

I have long been sensible that my library would be an interesting possession for the public, and the loss Congress has recently sustained, and the difficulty of replacing it, while our intercourse with Europe is so obstructed, [by war] renders this the proper moment for placing it at their service.[163]

Jefferson wrote the same thought to Monroe in Washington.[164] After much partisan squabbling in Congress—Jefferson never did lack enemies there—his library was purchased for $23,950, much below the actual cost of replacing the books on the open market.[165]

Although Jefferson must have felt some natural regret at parting with his beloved books, he must have been pleased that they would be preserved and used by his country, Koch believes.

He was excited by the thought that his library, which was recognized as the finest and most comprehensive collection of books in private hands in the United States, would nourish the minds of American statesmen, helping free them from bigotry.[166]

An editorial in Jefferson's time stated, "It is an honor to our country to say, that when a national collection was destroyed, the private library of a President could supply its place."[167]

While the Capitol was being rebuilt, Congress and its new library were both quartered in Blodget's Hotel. For a while the library was located in the attic of the Capitol, but by 1824, the "Library Hall" of the Capitol was finished. The Hall was considered by many people in Washington then to be "the most beautiful room, not only in the Capitol, but in the entire city of Washington."[168] In 1851 accidental fire broke out in the library, destroying two-thirds of the collection, so only a portion of Jefferson's actual library has been carefully preserved.[169]

Perhaps more important than the improvement of the physical facilities occasioned by Congress's acquiring Jefferson's library was the fact that Congress, for the first time, appointed a full-time librarian to have charge of its new library. The appointee was George Watterston, who gave Jefferson's books new book-plates and labels and published a catalog of the library based upon the one Jefferson had furnished. Watterston also used the arrangement of books and the classification scheme Jefferson had established.[170]

Jefferson, then, not only had an influence in selecting the first book collections for the use of Congress but also shaped the direction of the Library of Congress from its early beginnings in at least two important aspects. In the first place, the very nature of his own interests and his book collection which Congress acquired changed the library from a narrow, special reference collection to a large, general library befitting the broadening interests of Congress and the American nation. In the second place, Jefferson's ideas on librarianship and the classification and utilization of books were adopted by Watterston and so became part of the system used by the Library of Congress which has so much influenced librarianship in the United States. Jefferson sowed the seeds from which the Library of Congress grew into a great national library, probably the greatest in the world.

Jefferson's Activities as a Librarian

Jefferson's interest in librarianship has been noted even less than his interest in books and libraries, and very little in the way of comprehensive study has been done on this subject. Randolph Adams is one of the few scholars who has studied Jefferson as a librarian, publishing a short lecture on the subject in which he points out that many of the literary interests and skills which Jefferson displayed are necessary tools of the librarian. He notes, as other scholars have, Jefferson's unconcern with expensive special editions in favor of buying more usable books and adds:

> Not only did he buy books, and read books, but he had an amazingly retentive memory, a genius for selection, and a perfect passion for the systematic and orderly arrangement of data so as to make it readily available for actual use.[171]

Adams points out, as other scholars have, Jefferson's elaborate classification of his library by subjects to make its information more readily available.[172]

Other examples of Jefferson's careful library work are documented in his writings. John Adams wrote Jefferson that he had heard from a lady visitor to Jefferson's library that she had discovered "a large folio Volume on which was written 'libels' . . . which . . . [contained] Slips of newspapers, and pamphlets, vilifying . . . you."[173] Jefferson replied that he did have a volume of clippings on "personal altercations between individuals," but he had not thought the "volume of slanders" against himself worth reading, let alone preserving. He explained, "At the end of every year, I generally sorted all my pamphlets, and had them bound according to their subjects."[174]

Another example of Jefferson's librarian's instinct to collect information is seen in the commonplace notebooks of quotations, citations, and reflections on his studies which Jefferson began as a student and kept up during his later years, both as reference works and as means of preserving information on subjects he was interested in.[175] Even after he retired, Jefferson could refer to and quote from one of his "common-place books" on Anglo-Saxon law made when he was young and "bold in the pursuit of knowledge."[176]

Jefferson's biographers have noted how methodically he kept all sorts of accounts in his many notebooks, account books, farm books, garden books.[177] These records justified his librarian's instinct by proving to be important sources for later scholars to use. Peterson comments:

> He was fond of detail. His personal records—Account Book, Garden Book, Farm Book, and so on—exhibit a profusion of minutiae. He recorded from year to year, for instance, the exact time and place of planting a given vegetable, when it sprouted, when it ripened and came to the table. His meteorological observations, regularly three times a day, extended over several decades. All was neatly ordered and arranged.[178]

He had a librarian's passion for order and detail. Lehmann, in noting how methodically Jefferson kept notes and records and kept his library in order, comments:

He kept his affairs in order, those of his mind as well as those of his practical life. He had a garden book, and commonplace books, and collections of laws in manuscript. He kept his library in shape . . . with appropriate subdivisions for putting every book in its proper place so that he could easily find the sources of knowledge.[179]

As Lehmann points out, Jefferson was one of the eighteenth-century Enlightenment "encyclopedists" who felt the way to understand life and the world was to gather and digest more and more facts. Hence Jefferson's wide interests and investigations. Some detractors, Lehmann notes, have thought him a "superficial amateur who did a bit of everything, and nothing thouroughly." His studies, however, on a variety of subjects from government and morals to Indian and Anglo-Saxon vocabularies, were detailed and well done. Lehmann concludes that his "record of contributions to human civilization . . . [are] more valuable to his contemporaries and to posterity than that of most other men."[180]

Koch, in studying Thomas Jefferson as a philosopher, notes his interest in gathering information and in understanding both the natural and human world, which she believes qualifies him to be considered a philosopher, although she admits his antipathy to philosophic abstractions and systems.[181] She compromises by calling Jefferson "a true 'philosophe.'"

The "philosophe" [are] . . . men who are interested in ideas, in the latest findings of the sciences, in the increase of knowledge, but less from the point of view of technical exactness and . . . detail than from the angle of amateur systematic clarity and enthusiasm. The persistences of Jefferson's intellectual curiosity and its vast range of interest and inquiry are at once the keys to his personality and the sign of the "philosophe."[182]

What Lehmann and Koch do not seem to notice is that Jefferson's encyclopedic interest in knowledge and his "philosophe's" point of view are akin to a librarian's interest in collecting and using information. Adams is right in emphasizing Jefferson's scholarly interest in libraries:

His capacity for concentrated reading, digesting, and note taking was phenomenal. He did not arrive at his conclusions by introspection or intuition—they were all based on long and painstaking investigation and study.[183]

It is also possible, following Adams's suggestion, to see in Jefferson's varied literary activities the library functions carried out by most efficient libraries of today, although Jefferson naturally did not use the same terms.

Jefferson as a Reference Librarian. Jefferson was interested in gathering, preserving, classifying, using, and relating information both for his own use and for that of others. Adams comments, "Mr. Jefferson had that eternally investigative urge which ought to mark the reference librarian."[184] Jefferson was frequently consulted by correspondents to supply information, advice, and support for various publishing projects. One such library project that interested Jefferson was preserving the early legal code and statutes of Virginia, the oldest of the thirteen colonies. Jefferson spent years collecting, collating, and transcribing these and other early historical records, and it is due to his efforts that some were preserved in the Library of Congress.[185]

Adams seems to have been the first to notice that the type of books Jefferson most enjoyed writing were the reference works that librarians especially appreciate. Adams explains:

Another characteristic of librarians is their desire to compile hand-books. When he is frequently asked . . . questions on the same subject . . . he cannot resist the temptation to publish a volume which contains answers to the common enquiries, arranged in tabulated form. Mr. Jefferson's best-known book of this sort is *Notes on the State of Virginia.*[186]

Adams is quite right that Jefferson's book on Virginia is a reference-type work, written in the form of long answers to questions an intelligent foreigner might ask about the state of Virginia. It was first published in France for French readers when Jefferson was minister there.[187] A similar example is the revisions and articles he wrote for the French *Encylopédie Méthodique*.[188]

Nearly all of Jefferson's written works, in fact, are the type of works valued by librarians. Only his *Autobiography* is the type of original composition normally associated with authorship of books, and Jefferson himself said he wrote it with little interest "for my own more ready reference, and for the information of my family."[189] Many of his other writings were reference works of one type or another. *The Anas*, for example, was a collection of Jefferson's opinions, documents, and recollections of meetings and discussions that occurred while he was a member of George Washington's cabinet which he carefully preserved and published years later, "when the passions of the times had passed away."[190] Another reference work produced by Jefferson was *A Manual for Parliamentary Practice* which he wrote as a guide to use when, as vice-president of the United States, it was his task to preside over the Senate, since there were no set rules except the "decision of their President." Jefferson, in his usual thorough way, digested "the proceedings in the Senate, . . . the precepts of the Constitution, the regulations of the Senate, and where these are silent, of the rules of Parliament," complete with citations and explanations.[191] Even Jefferson's most famous works, his two versions of the New Testament, were "an abridgment of the New Testament . . . extracted from the account of his [Jesus'] life and doctrines as given by Matthew, Mark, Luke and John," as Jefferson described his first version, and "*The Morals and Life of Jesus of Nazareth* extracted textually from the Gospels in Greek, Latin, French, and English," as Jefferson described his second version.[192] These works again were reference works designed for handy use, rather than original discussions about Jesus.

Some scholars have noted, even in Jefferson's most important writings such as the Declaration of Independence and *A Summary of the Rights of British America*, a tendency to make a list of rights rather than to develop a philosophy of political science. Daniel Boorstin observes "A list of 'rights' substituted for a systematic theory of government."[193] This tendency corresponds to the point of view of many librarians, who are likely to list available information on a subject without forming their ideas into a philosophic system.[194]

[53]

Many of Jefferson's other writings are short essays on various subjects, some of them in outline form, such as his *Syllabus of the Doctrines of Epicurus* and *Syllabus of . . . the Merit of the Doctrines of Jesus.*[195] Such works likewise reveal Jefferson's librarian's interest in preparing handy reference material in abbreviated form.

The largest mass of Jefferson's writings is composed of his many speeches, addresses, replies to addresses, official opinions of governmental matters, and official and private letters. Jefferson was not vain enough to publish his addresses in collections, but he was careful to preserve for posterity copies of all his writings in such abundance that they have never all been gathered and published in one collection. Jefferson's concern for preserving irreplaceable reference material and documents again illustrates his appreciation of one of the most important functions of the librarian in society.

Jefferson's Readers' Advisory Service. Although Jefferson never used the term, it is evident that his interest in reading and education and his acknowledged expertise about books resulted in his frequently being consulted by his friends and acquaintances to provide advisory service on the choice of books to read on specified subjects or courses of study.

His several letters to various members of his extended family on the books to read and courses to study in their education, such as his letters to his nephew Peter Carr,[196] to his distant relative Francis Wayles Eppes,[197] and to his grandson Thomas Mann Randolph, Jr.,[198] are examples of Jefferson's providing advice about the best books to study in selected fields of knowledge. Although Jefferson's letters show a natural parental concern and gentle prodding to more studiousness, they also show a detailed knowledge of subject areas and offer summaries and advice about particular books, such as readers today seek from an expert librarian. In some cases Jefferson appended booklists of recommended reading.[199] Jefferson offered similar expert advice about the courses of study and authors to read or to avoid for the education of young women, gained from his educational experiences with his daughters.[200]

There is a striking similarity between the readers' advisory programs to recommend books for particular interests that libraries offer today and Jefferson's "direction of the studies of such young men as ask it . . . [who] have the use of my library and counsel."[201] Particularly in the field of law and the necessary general education preceding the study of law, Jefferson offered detailed reading guidance not only to Madison and Monroe, his disciples,[202] but to other aspiring lawyers and politicians, such as Phill Turpin[203] and Dabney Terrell.[204] He advised Dr. Thomas Cooper when he was "law-lecturer" on books to study,[205] and early in his career wrote a detailed course of books to read for the law and prelaw studies "of others . . . placed under my direction."[206]

Jefferson was just as proficient in recommending books for study in other fields. He laid out a whole course of reading in ancient and modern history for a professor of the newly opened University of Virginia and discussed each author in some detail.[207] When John Adams expressed an interest in studying the traditions and religion of the American Indians, Jefferson was able to suggest and discuss several books on the subject.[208]

Even more impressive than Jefferson's ability to advise individual readers on the best books to select on various subjects, were lists he drew up of recommended books on all the subjects necessary for a complete library. He was not only able to do this for an educated person's adequate personal library, listing a score or more of the best books on the subjects of "Fine Arts, Politicks and Trade, Religion, Law, Ancient History, Modern History, Natural Philosophy, Natural History,"[209] but he was able to suggest a whole library for the public officials of Congress which covered "History, Politics, Law, Treaties, War, Geography, Languages."[210] Perhaps Jefferson's most impressive feat as a librarian was to personally choose and classify the complete library for the new University of Virginia. As Honeywell points out:

> In Jefferson's list of books . . . there were 409 touching the classics, 367 on jurisprudence, 305 on modern history, 175 on religion and ecclesiastical history, 160 on pathology, 118 on philosophy and literature, and lesser numbers on other subjects. Many of these were in foreign languages. He classified them in forty-two groups.[211]

It is unlikely any single person has ever again performed such a feat of library selection.

Jefferson and Technical Processes. Confronted with the management and control of a library of several thousand volumes, Jefferson of necessity performed many of the functions of technical processing which in a modern library fall under the supervision of the librarian in charge of technical services. Jefferson, moreover, performed all the tasks himself as a labor of love, unlike William Byrd, another Virginian aristocrat of colonial times who collected a library somewhat comparable to Jefferson's but hired a tutor to care for his library in his spare time.[212]

Jefferson's own remarks indicate that he spent much of his leisure time selecting books, studying reviews, and keeping up with the latest publications. He wrote of spending much time in Paris bookstores "turning over every book with [his] own hand" and of having "standing orders during the whole time [he] was in Europe on its principal book-marts." He also wrote of "procuring" books after his return to America.[213] He had all the publishers' catalogues so he could select and order the books for the library of the University of Virginia.[214] His grandson, commenting on Jefferson's book interests after his retirement, said, "He . . . never missed the new number of a review, especially of the Edinburgh."[215] Jefferson indicated his interest in these sources of book reviews by allowing an article on his version of the New Testament and the teachings of Jesus to be published in this journal.[216]

Jefferson methodically kept up a newspaper and magazine file, for he mentioned to John Adams clipping and binding collections of articles, classified according to subject. "At the end of every year," he wrote, "I generally sorted all my pamphlets, and had them bound according to their subjects."[217] While he was president, Jefferson went on, he clipped and sent to his grandchildren "such morsels of poetry, or tales as I thought would please," teaching them to make scrapbooks to be kept in the library.[218] A younger granddaughter later recalled being taught this practice of good librarianship by her grandfather.[219]

In some of his letters to friends on book purchases Jefferson revealed that he was engaged in the work of librarianship. Reporting on his progress in obtaining books for Madison,

Jefferson wrote of conducting a "search for" a hard-to-get volume on Poland, of seeking to recover a "4th volume of D'Albon . . . lost by the bookbinder," and of planning to obtain a "reprint . . . of a scarce and excessively dear book."[220]

In Sowerby's extensive five-volume description of the books comprising the library Jefferson sold to Congress, she has provided not only the bibliographic information concerning each work but a physical description of each volume and any pertinent quotations from Jefferson's writings about ordering the work, evaluating its nature and content, or commenting on the author.[221] These descriptions provide many examples of Jefferson's painstaking technical work on his library. In the first part of the section on "Antient History" alone there are thirty-one examples of Jefferson's initialing the signatures of the books with I. and T., proving he habitually checked each book when he received it to be sure no pages or sections had been omitted.[222] He promptly let the bookseller know if he found anything missing.

In this small section of his library Jefferson had eight first editions,[223] the presence of which indicate his interest in collecting classical and important works rather than in collecting rare books since these works were used as hard as any others. Six of the books of this section had been specially bound for Jefferson, usually in small volumes to make them easy to handle.[224] In two cases Jefferson had gone to extra effort to try to obtain the smaller octavo edition of the work which he preferred for study.[225] In one case, when Thucydides' history of the Peloponnesian War had to be rebacked, Jefferson had an engraved map of Greece inserted.[226] Bookplates in three titles indicated Jefferson had bought them from other men's libraries, two of them being from that of William Byrd.[227] Jefferson's library had the same problem libraries today have of books not being returned, for one volume in this section was a late replacement copy purchased by Jefferson to complete the collection before sending it to the Congress.[228] Two of the volumes still had Jefferson's original classification and shelf marks pasted on the title page.[229]

Jefferson did not hesitate to have works bound to order to suit the special purpose of his library, which was study and comparison. The section on "Antient History" presents four examples of Jefferson's having two or more editions of the same work bound together for study, usually in Latin, Greek, and English translation. He even had his book bindery trim rare old editions to fit.[230] One famous example of Jefferson's unique rebinding of similar works was a collection of French memoirs of royal scandals which Jefferson had bound together in a set and titled "The Book of Kings." With dry humor Jefferson delighted in showing this work to visitors.[231]

Jefferson also was involved with the physical care of his books. He planned, helped build, and arranged the shelving of his library at Monticello.[232] When it was determined that Jefferson's library should be bought by Congress, he spent months numbering and arranging each book in its proper classification and position on the shelves.[233] He also saw to the packing, crating, and transporting of the books in their cases by wagon so that they would not be damaged and could be immediately set up in their proper place.[234] In his last years, Jefferson likewise partially unpacked, processed, and classified the books for the University of Virginia library.[235] All his life Thomas Jefferson was involved in being a librarian.

Jefferson and Circulation Regulations. Jefferson was concerned with the same conflicting purposes that perplex all circulation librarians, namely, that the works of the collection have the widest possible use and enjoy the greatest possible protection from loss or damage. The regulations he devised for the circulation of works from the libraries he developed reflect these concerns. In the small circulating county public libraries, which never got beyond the dreaming stage, he merely set the objectives for circulating "a few well-chosen books, to be lent to the people of the county, under such regulations as would secure their safe return in due time."[236]

In the case of the "Public" reference library in Richmond which Jefferson drew up as a proposed bill for the legislature to consider, he was more concerned with establishing a library board of three "visitors" to regulate the library, handle the funds, and hire the librarian than with the particular regulations of the library itself. He did provide that no person should "remove any book or map out of the said library, unless it be for necessary repair thereof." All of the items in the library should be made available for "the researches of the learned and curious, within the said library, without fee or reward." The "visitors" should make "rules for preserving them [the books and maps] safe and in good order."[237]

In the case of the library of the University of Virginia, a functioning reality, Jefferson drew up detailed regulations concerning the use of the library and the circulation of the collection. It is remarkable that many of his regulations are used by university libraries today. He provided that the faculty should have unlimited use of the books providing only that the books should be checked out with the librarian and that they should not be kept longer than "while in actual use."[238]

Knowing the carelessness of students, Jefferson provided more stringent regulations for their use of the library. Books had to be checked out by the librarian only, specific books should be loaned to particular students only by written permit from the student's professor, with the day of return determined. Only three books at a time could be borrowed and none taken "out of the precincts of the University." Fines were set for books kept overdue, and for books defaced or lost up to triple the cost of the book was to be charged. Rare or valuable books should not be lent to the students at all.[239]

The librarian's duties were also specified. He should have set hours and days to keep the library open to lend and receive books and should supervise the students' use of the library and their study there.

> The librarian shall make an entry of every book lent, and cancel the same when returned, so that it may always be known in what hands every book is. . . . To prevent derangement of the books, they [library users] are to take no book from the shelf but in his presence.

The librarian's salary was to be 150 dollars.[240] Jefferson himself appointed the first librarian and instructed him in the importance of his work in keeping the books and borrowers in order:

> It is incumbent . . . on yourself so to preserve the arrangement of the books under your care as never to disappoint

applicants by inability to find them. A library in confusion loses much of its utility.[241]

Jefferson thus early articulated the service aims of the circulation librarian.

Jefferson and Library Classification. Of all Jefferson's contributions to librarianship the one most noticed by scholars was the careful way he classified his own large library. Malone comments:

> He was not disposed to leave his books in disorder or to arrange them, as most people then did, primarily by their size. He preferred an arrangement by subject matter rather than one that was . . . alphabetical.[242]

Lehmann forther notes Jefferson's means and purpose of book classification:

> He kept his library in shape according to a rigid scheme based on Bacon's division of the three faculties of the human mind, reason, memory, and imagination, with appropriate subdivisions.[243]

Because Jefferson was one of the first in America to emphasize the importance of subject classification in libraries, Randolph Adams calls him "the father of American librarianship."[244]

The fact that Jefferson was so greatly concerned with the question of cataloging and classifying books is a good indication of his keen interest in librarianship, since the question is often a matter of indifference or mystery to most library users. As long as the collection is small, as in most private libraries, the owner may use any system of arrangement that seems desirable. Alistair Cooke, in a television program on the history of the United States, confessed that he arranged the books on the shelves of his library in an order similar to a map of the United States with those on Maine in the upper righthand corner, Florida in the lower corner, and California on the far left.[245] Since most of the early American libraries were small, it was customary to arrange them by the size of the editions, the accession order of their purchase, or alphabetically by author. James Servies points out that in 1773 the Harvard University Library and the catalog of its books were both arranged by alphabet, not subject, and the Dartmouth catalog and library in 1775 were arranged by size of books.[246] The Philadelphia Library Company was one of the first American libraries to publish a catalog of its holdings, in 1789, arranged by subjects based on Lord Bacon's "system of mental faculties because of dissatisfaction of its users with the confusion of its previous system."[247]

Jefferson, as usual, was ahead of his time. He was already practicing this latest literary theory before 1783 when he had leisure to bring the catalog of his library, which had by now grown to 2,640 volumes, up to date. This bound manuscript volume classifies his books by Lord Bacon's "table of sciences."[248] Jefferson's early interest in subject classification developed naturally from his desire to use his library for practical informational and educational purposes. As he expressed his opinion on "the subject of the arrangements of libraries" to George Watterston, librarian for the Library of Congress:

> Two methods offer themselves, the one alphabetical, the other according to the subject of the book. The former is very unsatisfactory, because of the medley it presents to the mind, the difficulty sometimes of recalling an author's name, and the greater difficulty, where the name is not given, of selecting the word in the title, which shall determine its alphabetical place. The arrangement according to subject is far preferable . . . because of the peculiar satisfaction, when we wish to consider a particular one, of seeing at a glance the books which have been written on it, and selecting those from which we effect most readily the information we seek.[249]

The idea of subject classification, which Jefferson pioneered in America, was not really a new idea since most large libraries over the years had followed that principle. Elmer Johnson has pointed out that ancient libraries, such as Ashurbanipal's huge library of clay tablets at Ninevah, were generally arranged by subject by rooms, one room being devoted to political records, one to religious legends and mythology, one to astronomy, one to medicine, and the like. Roman libraries were arranged according to general subjects, and catalogs were kept of the works by authors with the shelf position given. The chained libraries of the Medieval universities were generally classified according to the curriculum subject as taught in the universities. The great national libraries of Europe, such as the Bibliotheque Nationale and the British Library, are arranged by broad subject areas and by medium, such as manuscripts or printed works. In their shelf arrangements they are not, however, divided and subdivided by subjects to the extent that American libraries are, since sometimes an original royal or monastic library is kept intact.[250] There is a certain historic interest in being able to view King George II's personal library still elegantly displayed, the shelves arranged by book size. Extensive book catalogs and shelf position numbers are thus necessary for control of the collection.

The subject classification system that Jefferson adopted, he wrote to Watterston, "was formed . . . from Lord Bacon's table of science, modifying it to the changes in scientific pursuits which have taken place since his time, and to the greater or less extent of reading in the science which I proposed to myself."[251] Actually, Jefferson pointed out to another friend, the system had not originated with Bacon but "it had been proposed by Charron more than twenty years before in his book de la Sagesse."[252] One of the advantages of the system, Jefferson pointed out, was its flexibility.

> Thus the law having been my profession, and politics the occupation to which . . . the times . . . have called my particular attention, my provision of books in these lines . . . was more copious, and required . . . subdivisions into sections and paragraphs, while other subjects of which general views only were contemplated are thrown into masses.[253]

For a university, he wrote, "they will be grouped to coincide with kindred qualifications of Professors" and the curriculum.[254] He continued:

> Thus, in the library of a physician, the books of that science, of which he has many, will be subdivided under many heads;

THOMAS JEFFERSON, LIBRARIAN

and those of law, of which he has few, will be placed under a single one.[255]

Jefferson did not completely abandon the practice of arranging books according to size. Within the subject classifications, or "chapters" as he called them, he did not arrange his works alphabetically by author as is our practice today, although he generally grouped all the works of one author together.[256] As he explained to Watterston:

> In placing the books on their shelves, I have generally, but not always, collected distinctly the folios, quarto, octavo, and duodecimo, placing with the last all the smaller sizes.[257]

This practice meant that one had to rely solely on the catalog and the shelf position book number to locate the work.

> On every book is a label, indicating the chapter of the catalogue to which it belongs, and the other [order] it holds among those of the same format. So that, although the numbers seem confusing on the catalogue, they are consecutive on the volumes as they stand on their shelves, and indicate at once the place they occupy there.[258]

He made an alphabetical listing by authors at the end of the catalog.

Jefferson clearly attached great importance to the classifying and cataloging of his extensive library, since he spent much time at the task and even went to the expense of having his catalog printed.[259] The availability of this catalog was one of the advantages Jefferson stressed in offering his library for sale to Congress.[260] Its plan is given in table 1.

The scheme of classification which Jefferson charted for the catalog of his library in 1815 was essentially the same as the scheme he first devised for his library and catalog in 1783, the only difference being that he reduced the classes or "chapters" from forty-six to forty-four. When he developed the book classes for the catalog and library of the University of Virginia, he further simplified the categories to forty-two.[261]

The divisions and subdivisions of Jefferson's scheme were

[63]

TABLE 1
JEFFERSON'S CLASSIFICATION SCHEME AS PRINTED IN HIS 1815 CATALOGUE

Books may be classified according to the faculty of the mind employed on them: these are:

I. MEMORY   II. REASON   III. IMAGINATION
Which are applied respectively to:
I. HISTORY   II. PHILOSOPHY   III. FINE ARTS

					Chapter
		Civil Proper	Antient	....Antient History	1
	Civil		Modern	Foreign	2
				British	3
				American	4
		Ecclesiastical		Ecclesiastical	5
I. HISTORY				Natural Philosophy ...	6
				Agriculture	7
		Physics		Chemistry	8
				Surgery	9
				Medicine	10
	Natural	Natural History Proper	Animals	Anatomy	11
				Zoology	12
			Vegetables	......Botany	13
			Minerals	........Mineralogy	14
		Occupations of Man		Technical Arts	15
		Ethics		Moral Philosophy / Law of Nature and Nations	16
	Moral		Religious	Religion	17
				Equity	18
				Common Law	19
		Jurispru-dence	Municipal / Domestic	Law Merchant	20
				Law Maritime	21
II. PHILOSOPHY				Law Ecclesiastical ..	22
			Foreign	Foreign	23
			Oeconomical	Politics	
				Commerce	24
	Mathematical	Pure		Arithmetic	25
				Geometry	26
				Mechanics	
				Statics	
				Dynamics	
		Physico-Mathematical		Pneumatics	27
				Phonics	
				Optics	
				Astronomy	28
				Geography	29

quite awkward and never occupied an important part in the classification work of his library. By striving to make his book classifications part of a complete tree of knowledge based on

[64]

TABLE 1—Continued

III. Fine Arts			Chapter
	Architecture	Architecture	30
	Gardening	Gardening	
	Painting	Painting	31
	Sculpture	Sculpture	
	Music	Music	32
	Poetry	Epic	33
		Romance	34
		Pastorals	
		Odes	35
		Elegies	
		Didactic	36
		Tragedy	37
		Comedy	38
		Dialogue	
		Epistles	39
	Oratory	Logic	
		Rhetoric	40
		Orations	
	Criticism	Theory	41
		Bibliography	42
		Languages	43
Authors who have written on various branches		Polygraphical	44

SOURCE: Sowerby, *Catalogue*, 1:xi.

Lord Bacon's "ascription of the sciences to these respective faculties . . . of the mind,"[262] some very unusual subdivisions were created. The first classification of ancient history under the ancient subdivision of the civil proper division of civil history, placed under the human faculty of memory is understandable, but it seems odd to present-day readers to place ecclesiastical history under the division of civil history, so far has Jefferson's goal of disestablishing the church and separating religious history and law from civil history and law been accomplished. It also seems odd to classify the sciences under "Natural History" and mathematics under "Pure Mathematical Philosophy," until one remembers that Jefferson was following Bacon's suggestion of separating all classes according to whether they primarily used man's "memory" or his "reason." Jefferson's classifications under the division of fine arts based on the human faculty of "imagination" is simpler and more understandable today (see table 1).

In Jefferson's defense, it must be said that these subdivisions were no more exaggerated for his time than some of the subdivisions of the Dewey Decimal Classification system today which, to take but one example among many, assigns the subject of "houseboats" to the subdivisions of "architecture, engineering, or interior decoration," depending on the judgment of the cataloger concerning the main emphasis of the book.[263] It is also true that many differences of classification necessarily reflect changes in the interests of society. The fact that Jefferson devoted a whole classification to "Epic poetry" alone, while Dewey makes "Poetry, Epic" a subdivision under "Collections" under "Literature,"[264] indicates a shift in emphasis and in the study of classic poetry.

Some of Jefferson's book classifications, moreover, were due to his own interests. Since the law was his "profession" and politics his "occupation,"[265] he had many separate classes of books for different types of law under the division of "Municipal Jurisprudence" but he put "Gardening, Painting, and Sculpture" all into one class under "Fine Arts" since he had few books on fine arts and his interest was largely confined to the development of formal gardens (see table 1). The flexibility of his scheme of classification and its adaptability to the "particular pursuits of a lawyer, . . . physician or theologoist [sic]" were some of its advantages, Jefferson pointed out to Watterston.[266]

Most of the oddities of Jefferson's system of classification arose not in the book classes he devised "to throw convenient masses of books under each separate head,"[267] but in the branching tree of knowledge uniting the tables of science which he adapted from Bacon. One must remember that Jefferson was absorbed in the larger Enlightenment interests of classifying, understanding, and relating various new discoveries in the emerging branches of science, which were then in their infancy, and that his library was an important tool for the greater purpose of understanding the Creator's world of nature and of human society. Jefferson discussed the importance of classifying knowledge in a letter to John Manners on "methods of classification adopted by different writers on Natural History." Although Jefferson modestly apologized for having been too busy with "civil concerns" to have gained an expert knowledge of natural science, he proceeded to show familiarity with the studies of species done by "Ray," "Klein," and "Brisson . . . till Linnaeus appeared."

Fortunately for science, he conceived in the three kingdoms of nature, modes of classification which obtained the approbation of the learned of all nations. His system was accordingly adopted by all. . . . It offered the three great desiderata: First, of aiding the memory to retain a knowledge of the productions of nature. Secondly, of rallying all to the same names for the same objects, so that they could communicate understandingly on them. And, thirdly, of enabling them, when a subject was first presented, to trace it by its character up to the conventional name by which it was agreed to be called.[268]

Using this discussion as his authority, Servies argues that Jefferson, in his Baconian library classification system, was trying to do more than classify books; he was trying to classify science and all knowledge. The larger purposes of Jefferson's library classification, Servies believes, were the same as those Jefferson attributed to Linnaeus's system for the natural sciences, namely, as an aid to memory, as an aid to the description of natural phenomena, and as an aid in the communication of knowledge between scientists.[269]

Another reason for some of the peculiarities of Jefferson's classifications was the undeveloped stage of certain sciences. Geology, he explained, he put under "Mineralogy" where what was useful and factual about "stratification, collection and sequence of the different species of rocks and other mineral substances" would naturally come. Jefferson had no place for the theories of geology concerning "the self-generation of the universe, or . . . of our own globe by the agency of water, fire, or . . . the fiat of the Creator."[270] Jefferson also purposely made no provision for the controversial theories of different schools of medicine or the "multifarious creeds" of religion. He had little use for metaphysical speculation and so "incorporated Metaphysics with Ethics, [with] little extension given to them"[271]

By making his library classification system part of this elaborate theory of knowledge, Jefferson incurred the disadvantages of a forced simplification of the fields of learning, and a certain vagueness and inelasticity. These factors eventually led to radical modification of the system by both the Library of Con-

gress and the library of the University of Virginia both of which
adopted the system from Jefferson, although, according to Harry
Clemons, for many years head librarian of the University of
Virginia Library, this change was long in coming.[272] The
fact that Jefferson's system was used with only "slight modifica-
tions . . . until the turn of the present century" by these two
important libraries indicates Jefferson's importance as a librarian, Servies concludes from his study.[273] Goodrum comments
in his study of the Library of Congress today:

> [When the first] Librarian locked . . . Jefferson's . . .
> forty-four subject divisions into a printed book catalogue,
> . . . [he] froze the Library of Congress's classification scheme
> for a hundred years. As late as Theodore Roosevelt's time,
> the Library's catalogers were dutifully sorting hundreds of
> thousands of volumes into the same forty-four compart-
> ments in which the earliest titles had sat on the shelves at
> Monticello.[274]

Actually, the philosophical table of human knowledge was
not an integral part of Jefferson's library classification system
and it was quite possible to use Jefferson's book classes or
"chapters" apart from the theoretical divisions and subdivisions.
Over the years, both Jefferson and the library's users tended to
simplify. A comparison of the classification scheme used by
Jefferson for his library catalog of 1815 with the one he used
for the catalog of the new library of the University of Virginia
which, he wrote Madison in 1824, he had finally "got through
. . . except the alphabet" clearly reveals this trend.[275]

The classification for the University of Virginia still used
the same main divisions of "History, Philosophy, and Fine
Arts" based on the faculties of "Memory, Reason, and Imagination" which resulted in virtually the same book classes (see table
2). Only a few minor simplifications took place in book classes.
A wholesale simplification and improvement of the intervening
divisions and subdivisions, however, took place. History was
divided simply into two classes, "Civil" which took in the
history of nations and peoples, and "Physical" which covered
the sciences. The subdivisions and divisions of the 1815 catalog,
such as "Animals, Vegetables, and Minerals" under "Natural

TABLE 2
JEFFERSON'S CLASSIFICATION SCHEME
FOR THE LIBRARY OF THE UNIVERSITY OF VIRGINIA

Books are addressed to the three faculties of

MEMORY		REASON		IMAGINATION
		to these belong respectively		
HISTORY		PHILOSOPHY		FINE ARTS
Civil	Physical	Mathematical	Moral	
1. Ancient	6. Physics,	17. Arithmetic	19. Ethics	29. Architecture
2. Modern,	pure and	18. Geometry	20. Religion	Gardening
Foreign	mixed		21. Law—	30. Painting
3. Modern,	7. Agricul-		Nature and	Sculpture
British	ture		Nations	Music
4. Modern,	8. Chemistry		22. Law of Equity	31. Poetry, Epic
American	9. Anatomy		23. Law Common	32. Poetry, Romance
5. Modern,	Surgery		24. Law Merchant	33. Poetry, Pastoral
Ecclesi-	10. Medicine		25. Law Maritime	34. Poetry, Didactic
astical	11. Zoology		26. Law Ecclesi-	35. Poetry, Tragedy
	12. Botany		astical	36. Poetry, Comedy
	13. Mineralogy		27. Law Foreign	37. Poetry, Dialogue
	14. Technics		28. Politics	and Epistolary
	15. Astronomy			38. Rhetoric
	16. Geography			39. Criticism, Theory
				40. Criticism, Bibliography
				41. Criticism, Philology
		42. Polygraphical		

SOURCE: Thomas Jefferson, "A Catalogue of Books Forming the Body of a Library for the University of Virginia," first printed in the University of Virginia, *Alumni Bulletin* (November, 1895) 79-80; in Padover, *Complete Jefferson*, pp. 1091-93.

History Proper," were eliminated entirely. In a similar fashion, in the university catalog "Philosophy" was divided simply into the two divisions of "Mathematical and Moral" and the complications of the subdivisions of "Domestic, Municipal, Jurisprudence" and "Physico-Mathematical" of the 1815 catalog were eliminated (compare tables 1 and 2).

Evidence that Jefferson himself did not bother with these elaborate complications is seen in a letter he wrote to a friend instructing him in the use of his library at Monticello while Jefferson was away. He explained the book classification scheme in this brief way:

The arrangement is as follows: 1. Antient history. 2. Modern do. 3. Physics. 4. Natural History proper. 5. Technical arts. 6. Ethics. 7. Jurisprudence. 8. Mathematics. 9. Gardening, architecture, sculpture, painting, music, poetry. 10. Oratory. 11. Criticism. 12. Polygraphical. You will find this on a paper nailed up somewhere in the library.[276]

Jefferson went on to explain shelf location in the two rooms that housed his library in this unique way:

> The arrangement begins behind the partition door leading out of the Bookroom into the Cabinet, and proceeds from left to right round the room; then entering the Cabinet it begins at the eastern angle, and goes round that room. The presses not having sufficed to contain the whole, the latter part of polygraphics was put into the kind of closet at the first entrance of the book-room.[277]

The fact that Jefferson had a true librarian's concern to control the circulation of his books is seen in the fact that, while he freely gave permission for his friend to have the key to the house and the use of the library, he requested him "to note on . . . a piece of paper on one of the tables of the room . . . the books you have occasion to take out, and to blot it out when returned . . . so that should I want a book at any time when at home, I may know where it is." He also showed a librarian's attention to book location:

> As after using a book, you may be at a loss in returning it to its exact place, and they cannot be found again when misplaced, it will be better to leave them on a table in the room. My familiarity with their places will enable me to replace them readily.[278]

Jefferson, indeed, had all the instincts of the true librarian concerning the importance of books and the importance of adequate library systems of classifying and controlling a book collection. The fact that he was more interested in the classification of books than in a philosophical system of knowledge is revealed by his statement to Woodward:

Your idea of making the subject matter of the sciences the basis of their distribution, is certainly more reasonable than that of the faculties to which they are addressed.[279]

Randolph Adams points out that Jefferson's great contribution to librarianship was that he bridged the gap between philosophers such as Aristotle and Bacon, who sought to classify all human learning, and later librarians.

The noteworthy fact is that Jefferson thought of the classification in terms of books, even though his system was based on a classification of knowledge. If some of his subdivisions seem a little odd today, that is not important. The point is that he made a contribution, as important in its way as Dr. Franklin's discovery of electricity.[280]

Indeed, the part of Jefferson's classification scheme that was most valuable and enduring was the part he devised, the book classes, while the part that was most dated and soonest discarded was the classification of learning that he took from Bacon.

Servies also emphasizes the contribution of Jefferson to our American system of library classification and information retrieval. He writes, "To bridge the gap between the Englishman, Sir Francis Bacon, and the American Melvil Dewey, this work of the third president of the United States, Thomas Jefferson, deserves the greatest consideration."[281] He concludes his study of Jefferson's work of bibliographic classification with this estimate:

The very nature of Jefferson's early scheme of American book classification . . . and its successors, employed far after the death of its author, indicates clearly that it is one of the most outstanding classifications in early American libraries, when judged by the continuity of its use, by the importance of those libraries which employed it, and by the stature of its author.[282]

Jefferson's Broader Library Interests. True librarians are interested in more important matters than the mechanical details of controlling a book collection. Jefferson in particular was concerned with many of the deeper issues of the place of libraries in society and their role in the education of man for the free, democratic life.

One instance was Jefferson's concern, similar to that of many librarian's today, with the excessive cost of important scholarly works on the American market which put them beyond the reach of most students and many libraries. As Jefferson explained in a letter to a friend, the Congress had placed a duty on books from abroad in order to encourage the American publishing business. Only the cheapest and most popular works were found to be profitable for American printers, however. Jefferson wrote:

> For the editions of value, enriched by notes, commentaries, etc. and for books in foreign living languages, the demand here is too small and sparse to reimburse the expense of re-printing them. . . . The duty on them becomes consequently not a protecting, but really a prohibitory one.[283]

Although seminaries could get an exemption from the duty,[284] the duty was a hardship on students and a detriment to the advancement of libraries and learning. Jefferson, accordingly, engaged in a letter-writing compaign to convince Congress "in their wisdom to see its impolicy." He argued, "To prohibit us from the benefit of foreign light, is to consign us to long darkness."[285]

Another concern Jefferson shared with modern librarians was for the preservation of books as the record of society for future study. He showed his concern not only by encouraging others to write history but by diligently preserving primary source material of the history in which he was involved. Few presidents have spent as much time as he did preserving, collating, and arranging his letters and documents for future historical research.[286]

Because of his belief in the importance of libraries as the depositories of the knowledge of mankind, Jefferson felt the same indignation most librarians feel over the burning of books. He wrote scathingly to Adams about the burning of the Library of Congress by the British during the War of 1812, referring to "the devastations of British Vandalism at Washington."[287] He also wrote to a friend in Congress:

> I learn from the newspapers that the vandalism of our enemy has triumphed at Washington over science as well as the arts, by the destruction of the public library with the noble edifice in which it was deposited. Of this transaction, as of that of Copenhagen, the world will entertain but one sentiment . . . [concerning these] acts of barbarism which do not belong to a civilized age.[288]

In their correspondence Jefferson and Adams lamented over the destruction and suppression of books and libraries over the centuries by "Priests and Despots" of every period and faith, from the destruction of the Alexandrian library and "the craft, the power and the profit of the priests" of the Middle Ages to the "disposition of Democrats, Rebells and Jacobins . . . both to destroy and to forge Records."[289]

Another issue that concerned Jefferson and often disturbs librarians was book censorship. Jefferson usually saw the problem as part of the larger issue of freedom of thought, particularly religious freedom, and freedom from political tyranny. The cause of intellectual freedom, for which Jefferson did so much, was an important part of the Enlightenment struggle for religious freedom and political liberty. The struggle to prevent the censorship of books and individual thought, whether by governmental action or public opinion, was a fundamental cause with Jefferson.[290] It was this larger cause of intellectual freedom which aroused his eloquent statement, "I have sworn upon the altar of God, eternal hostility against every form of tyranny over the mind of man."[291]

On at least one occasion, however, Jefferson went on record against the censorship of books themselves. Jefferson had subscribed to a French book "On the Creation of the World" as a routine matter of book selection for his collection on astronomy or geology. The work turned out to be an attack on the Newtonian philosophy.[292] The Philadelphia bookseller who handled the importation of the book for Jefferson was prosecuted by the civil magistrate for selling an irreligious book.[293] Jefferson wrote indignantly:

> I am really mortified to be told that, *in the United States of America* . . . a question about the sale of a book can be

carried before the civil magistrate. Is this then our freedom
of religion? And are we to have a censor whose imprimatur
shall say what books may be sold, and what we may buy?
. . . Is a priest to be our inquisitor, or shall a layman,
simple as ourselves, set up his reason as the rule for what
we are to read, and what we must believe?[294]

As Jefferson dryly commented, Newton did not need any defense
by the magistrate, "and still less [does] the holy Author of our
religion."

> It is an insult to our citizens to question whether they are
> rational beings or not, and blasphemy against religion to
> suppose it cannot stand the test of truth and reason. If M.
> de Becourt's book be false in its facts, disprove them; if false
> in its reasoning, refute it. But, for God's sake, let us freely
> hear both sides, if we choose.[295]

Jefferson not only proclaimed the basic principle of opposing
censorship so that the truth may be found by freely examining
all sides of an issue, but he also practiced intellectual freedom
in his use of books. Bestor points to Jefferson's way of dealing
with certain important books with which he disagreed as a model
of how librarians in a democratic society should meet the issue
of censorship:

> Three great and influential books of the eighteenth century
> interested Jefferson and yet disturbed him. One was Mon-
> tesquieu's *Spirit of Laws*, another was David Hume's *History
> of England*, the third was Blackstone's *Commentaries on
> the Laws of England*. Each was a masterpiece of its kind.
> . . . Each was in Jefferson's library and each was carefully
> studied by him.[296]

Yet each of these books inculcated points of view that Jefferson
opposed. Montesquieu was too enamored of the British constitution and too fearful of democracy, Hume's charming history
was too favorable to the British royalty, Blackstone's useful
summary of British law had a Tory bias which made American
law students and politicians too conservative. Jefferson's solu-

tion was not to censor or suppress these works but to seek other works of opposing points of view and to go back to original sources.[297] Jefferson thoroughly enjoyed and vigorously took part in debate. As Bestor states, "The American Republic was not created by and cannot be preserved by men who are afraid of ideas."[298]

Jefferson's way of fearlessly seeking the truth by freely examining all ideas remains the only course the library in a democratic society can take. Bestor concludes:

> Many groups of citizens . . . are concerned about libraries. It is proper that they should be. But they ought to search the shelves, not to unearth an occasional volume containing aberrant ideas, but to discover whether the basic books that embody the essence of the American tradition are universally available. Let patriotic groups inaugurate campaigns, not to remove certain books from our libraries, but to place certain books there. . . .
>
> The negative way of defending freedom is monstrously futile. . . .
>
> This is not liberty and enlightenment. It is emptiness and gloom. . . . Who ever heard of pulling down the shades to shut out the darkness? Our salvation is to light the lamps and to keep them burning.[299]

At the forefront of the battle for freedom, enlightenment, and truth was Thomas Jefferson, firm in his faith that man and his world embodied the Creator's wisdom. It is not surprising Americans today find instruction in a renewed study of Jefferson.

Summary and Conclusions

Although comparatively few studies have been made of Jefferson's library activities, most scholars have noticed his keen interest in reading and his extensive book collecting. Jefferson wrote about himself, "I was a hard student until I entered on the business of life, . . . and now, retired, . . . I am again a hard student."[300] He had more than his share of intellectual curiosity, regarded reading as a "canine pleasure" and retained and digested his reading well.

All of his life he used much of his leisure for selecting and collecting books from booksellers all over the world. These books he formed into not one but several extensive personal libraries for his own use and that of his friends. He spent much time classifying and arranging his libraries by an intricate system of subject classification, based on an elaborately branching tree of knowledge taken from Bacon's "tables of sciences." Although the philosophical theories behind Jefferson's classification system were soon outmoded, the subject classifications he developed were the basis of the system used by the Library of Congress and the library of the University of Virginia, which Jefferson helped found, for eighty-three years after his death.[301] "[This] contirbution [was] as important in its way as Dr. Franklin's discovery of electricity," concludes Randolph Adams.[301]

Because of his belief in the importance of the role libraries could play in educating free men for self-government and self-development, Jefferson was active throughout his life in promoting the development of public libraries. He advocated the establishment of county public libraries in Virginia and a state library at Richmond soon after the Revolution. Jefferson was active in early steps to establish a library for the use of Congress. When the Congressional library was destroyed by the British burning of Washington during the War of 1812, he sold his own personal library, one of the finest and most extensive then in existence in America, to Congress as a replacement. Jefferson's library was the real beginning of the Library of Congress, making Jefferson's library work most influential upon American librarianship. Jefferson's influence was also extended through his work in selecting, ordering, and classifying the books for the library of the University of Virginia, and in establishing its library regulations. Harry Clemons, director of the University of Virginia Library for twenty-three years, comments:

> Thomas Jefferson was a potent figure in the establishment of both . . . the . . . Library of Congress and of this . . . University Library in the Commonwealth . . . ; he appointed the first two Librarians of each; each Library has developed from nucleus collections which were selected by him personally; and in the arrangement of its collections

each Library followed his classification scheme practically throughout the nineteenth century.[303]

Throughout his life Jefferson carried on many of the activities of the modern professional librarian. Nearly all of the books he wrote were compiled as reference-type works to provide useful information. His book *Notes on Virginia* was designed to acquaint foreigners with America. His *Parliamentary Manual* was compiled to provide guidance for conducting the business of the United States Senate. His versions of selected passages from the New Testament were designed for personal devotions and study.

Jefferson gave freely of his time and knowledge in advising family and friends on books to read and courses of study to pursue. His knowledge of books was so extensive that he was able to design the entire curriculum and necessary reading lists for the creation of the University of Virginia.

A study of Jefferson's private library at Monticello, which grew to seven or eight thousand volumes, reveals that he was well aware of the importance of the technical processes necessary to make his collection useful. Jefferson carefully inspected and collated each new book, classified it, assigned it a shelf position and book number, and recorded it in his library catalog. He was generous in loaning books to friends but kept a careful record of who borrowed each book. The regulations Jefferson established for the circulation and care of the University of Virginia Library were very similar to library regulations practiced by modern university libraries for the control of their collections today.

Jefferson was also active in promoting the larger causes that concern librarians today. He worked to lower the costs of good books and make them more available to students. He saw the importance of preserving historical material for future study, and collected such an immense amount of primary source material about the history in which he took part that Jefferson's materials have never been fully edited. The burning of books and the destruction of priceless libraries filled him with the same dismay it does librarians today.

Jefferson was outspoken against censorship and any limitations on intellectual and religious freedom. Both religion and science could stand the test of truth, and truth could best be established by free discussion, he argued. Neither "Newton" nor "the holy Author of our religion" needed any defense by the "magistrate," Jefferson wrote in connection with a civil action against a bookseller who imported an "irreligious" book for him.[304] Jefferson conducted a lifelong crusade against any "tyranny over the mind of man."[305]

Books were, for Jefferson, the necessary ammunition in the war against ignorance and tyranny to free the mind of man for a destined place of happiness in the Creator's world. Libraries were the important means of making books, the tool for man's advance, available. As Malone concludes:

> No American of his generation . . . did so much to empha-
> size the sacred freedom of the human spirit and the necessary
> nourishment of the mind [by] . . . the supreme importance
> . . . of books.[306]

3

Jefferson's Library

IT IS A COMMON belief that a person can tell a good deal about the interests and character of a friend by browsing through the books and magazines he has in his home. What can one tell, then, about Thomas Jefferson from browsing through his library? Is it true that as a typical Virginian and intellectual son of the Enlightenment he was less interested in religion than his contemporaries from New England? As a lawyer, statesman, and politician was he more interested in government and law than the average person? Coming from a small, far colony of Great Britain was he provincial in his outlook? As an aristocratic slave owner was he conservative in his social point of view? As a manager of several plantations was he interested in farming and building or was that beneath him? Was he interested in social pleasures and what did he do for recreational reading? These are but a few of the questions that may be answered by examining the reading interests revealed in Jefferson's library. Koch comments from her study of Jefferson's reading, "Since his library was the product of extraordinary devotion and, as he said, 'hand-picked,' it is a valuable index to his intellectual attachments."[1]

Even a cursory examination of Jefferson's thought and library reveals that here was no social dilettante but a serious scholar. His library had little fiction and his collection of belles lettres was all good literature. Although Jefferson complained of

[79]

the poor quality of education at William and Mary College which he attended—it was "filled . . . with children [who were] learners of Latin and Greek," he said—it is evident Jefferson himself obtained a good education.[2] Modern college students with a year or two of a foreign language would be impressed with the many volumes in Greek, Latin, French, and Spanish in Jefferson's library which he read fluently. He found reading works in the original language a great pleasure.[3] Norman Cousins draws these conclusions from Jefferson's library:

> If a man is known by the books he reads and keeps, then the library at Monticello can tell us a great deal about Thomas Jefferson. There are sections on art, architecture, music, history, science, poetry, belles-lettres, religion, and philosophy.[4]

Koch believes "the preponderance of books" in Jefferson's library reflects "his deep intellectual interests:"

> They range . . . from classics first, to jurisprudence, modern history, religion, pathology, philosophy, . . . literature, and lesser numbers on other subjects.[5]

Subject Analysis of Jefferson's Libraries

The *William and Mary Quarterly* has published various articles on the subject of Thomas Jefferson and his libraries. One of the most helpful is by William Peden, who describes and compares the subject contents of three libraries Thomas Jefferson collected: (1) the "great" library which he spent most of his life collecting and sold to Congress, (2) the smaller one he subsequently collected for "the amusements of . . . his old age," and (3) the one he bought as regent for the new University of Virginia.[6]

Peden finds history comprised the largest section in all three libraries: Jefferson's main library had over 599 works on ancient and modern history, his "old-age" library had 166, fifty more than in any other field, and the university library chosen by Jefferson had "300 books in modern history alone, which, when added to the number of books on ancient history, again places this field at the head of any list of Jefferson's interests." Among his favorite authors were Herodotus, Tacitus, Caesar, Hume, Robertson, and Gibbon.[7]

Jefferson's keen interest in history is quite understandable. As a leader in the struggle for American independence, he had an early interest in the study of American and British history to provide justification for the battle with the British crown. His long life of public service deepened his interest in contemporary history. His early classical education, on the other hand, gave him an abiding interest in the history of ancient Greece and Rome. After his retirement from the struggles of politics he expressed a preference for ancient history over current affairs:

> I read no newspaper now but Ritchie's, and in that chiefly the advertisements, for they contain the only truths to be relied on in a newspaper. I feel a much greater interest in knowing what has passed two or three thousand years ago, than in what is now passing. I read nothing, therefore, but of the heroes of Troy, of the wars of . . . Athens, of . . . Caesar and of Augustus too, the Bonaparte and parricide scoundrel of that day.[8]

Since Jefferson was deeply influenced by the ideals and philosophy of the Enlightenment from his college days on, he preferred the history and culture of ancient Greece and Rome to that of medieval Europe. Enlightenment philosophers looked to the golden age of Athens and republican Rome as an inspiration in their struggle against the tyranny and prejudice of church and crown.[9] Hence the importance of the study of ancient history.

It was also a belief of the Enlightenment and of Jefferson and his contemporaries that a study of history, particularly of the classical age, would provide guidance in forming new answers to the pressing religious, social, and political issues of freedom and self-rule. Jefferson accordingly urged the study of history in his various proposals of education and believed works on history were most important in the book collections of the various libraries he suggested.[10] In a letter to a member of the faculty of the University of Virginia, Jefferson related his favorite works and authors for ancient history:

In all cases I prefer original authors to compilers. . . .
I should advise the usual suite of Herodotus, Thucydides,
Xenophon, Diodorus, Livy, Caesar, Suetonius, Tacitus,
and Dion, in their originals if understood, and in translations if not.[11]

Evidence that Jefferson read the works he recommended is found
in the fact that Sowerby found these titles as important parts
of Jefferson's library.[12]   Jefferson went on to recommend the
works of Gibbon and Segus[13] to sum up history. He suggested
other lesser works could be read at leisure, recommending
"Polybius, Sallust, Plutarch,"[14] and others. He also thought
a good general reference work on "ancient universal history
should be on our shelves."[15]

   In studying modern history, Jefferson believed it was important for Americans "to be intimately acquainted [with] . . . but
two nations . . . France and England." For the study of
France, Jefferson recommended a "succession of particular
history . . . making up [for] the general one which they
want."[16]   Among the historical works he recommended were
Millot's general history of France and the works of Davila,
Perefixe, Sully, and Voltaire's *Louis XIV and XV*,[17] Marmontel's *Regence*, and Foulongion's *French Revolution*.[18]

   For the history of England Jefferson recommended the works
of Rapin, Ludlow, Fox, Belsham, Hume and Brodie.[19] Rapin
he praised for his scope and faithfulness but admitted its difficulty. Hume's work he praised as "the finest piece of history
which has ever been written . . . were it faithful," and discussed
at some length the way Hume was biased in his accounts because
of his favoring the rights of the sovereigns of England over
those of the people. For general accounts of modern history
Jefferson also recommended "Russell's *Modern Europe*, Robertson's *Charles V*,[20] Mollet's *Northern Antiquities*, . . . Millot's
Modern History, Hallam's *Middle Ages*."[21]

   Reflecting Jefferson's interest in law, the next largest section
to history was his collection on legal subjects. Peden counted
450 books on law in his main library, 370 in the university
library, and 64 in his retirement library. Among the authors
noted by Peden were Kame's *Principles of Equity*, Purvis' *Laws*

of Virginia, Blackstone's *Commentaries,* Coke's *Entries,* Henning's *Statutes at Large.*[22]

On occasion Jefferson discussed the best works of law to study with lawyer friends or with students seeking his guidance in their legal studies. He noted that there were four basic digests of English law to study:[23] Bracton's *De Legibus Angliae,* Coke's *Institutes,* Matthew Bacon's *Abridgment of the Law,* and *Blackstone's Commentaries.*[24] The difficulty was that Bracton's work was in "antiquated Latin," Coke's work was in "chaotic form," and Bacon's work was important but not authoritative.[25] Blackstone's work was well organized and made the study of law easier. Hence it came into great vogue for the study of law in America, but it had an unfortunate proaristocratic, antirepublican bias which was prejudicing American lawyers and politicians, Jefferson believed.[26] The best work for students,[27] Jefferson found, was a new edition of Coke's *Institutes* by Thomas who edited the material into more usable form.[28] After all these studies were mastered, the law student could go on to the study of law specialities, such as "Admiralty law, Ecclesiastical law, and the Law of Nations."[29] It was not surprising Jefferson had so many works on so many different law headings in his libraries. He was clearly an expert on law.

Another large part of Jefferson's libraries was his section on politics. Peden reports:

> If Jefferson was first a lawyer, he was next a statesman and politician, and his interests as such are mirrored in his libraries. His greatest collection contained 450 books concerning theories of government, politics, statecraft, and political economy; his last library 106; and the library for the University of Virginia 170. Among these were the works of such writers as Condorcet, Diderot, Hobbes, Locke, Hume, Montesquieu, Destutt de Tracy, Dugald Stewart, Jeremy Bentham, Smith's *Wealth of Nations,* Malthus on *Population,* Godwin's *Politican Justice,* More's *Utopia,* and Priestly.[30]

It can be readily seen that, although Jefferson kept and filed works and materials on partisan political issues and conflicts, he was thinking of politics in the broader sense encompassing political and social science. Jefferson and his friends of the Enlightenment were much concerned with philosophies of government,[31] the true origin of society, the natural rights of men,[32] the moral and legal basis for human freedom, and the basis of organizing a republican government. Particularly in the United States the need to organize such new governments to replace the colonial systems was pressing. Hence Jefferson's interest in the political and social theorists named by Peden.

Jefferson's works on politics illustrate the extensive use he made of reading to provide him with the ideas and materials for his work as a statesman and lawyer. He studied the works well, critically digesting and revising them in the light of his own experience and thought. He took extensive notes on Montesquieu's *Spirit of Laws*, for example, but disagreed with many parts. He wrote to his friend Destutt de Tracy, who published a revision of Montesquieu, as follows:

> I had, with the world, deemed Montesquieu's work of much merit; but saw in it, with every thinking man, so much of paradox, of false principle and misapplied fact, as to render its value equivocal on the whole. . . . [Your] radical correction of them, therefore, was a great desideratum.[33]

Another example of Jefferson's criticism of the works of authors in his library is contained in Jefferson's letter to a young relative whose education he was guiding:

> You ask my opinion of Lord Bolingbroke and Thomas Paine. They were alike in making bitter enemies of the priests and pharisees of their day. Both were honest men; both advocates for human liberty. . . . These two persons differed remarkable in the style of their writing, each leaving a model of what is most perfect in both extremes of the simple and the sublime.[34]

Commenting on the section of Jefferson's libraries containing the lighter works of fiction and imagination, the "belles-lettres," Peden notes Jefferson had the essays of Addison and Steele, the novels of Fielding, the works of Shakespeare, and the works of

Milton (Jefferson's major library contained four editions of
Milton, including a "first edition in ten books"[35]). Peden also
comments on the heavy classical interest reflected in the collection. Jefferson had 300 works of poetry, drama, and romance
in Latin and Greek, featuring such authors as Homer, Aeschylus,
and Virgil.[36]

Peden notes that Jefferson had very few novels in his library
and did not have the taste for "romances" that his friend John
Adams confessed to.[37] Peden comments:

> Thomas Jefferson was a man who usually indulged in
> no high flights of the imagination, and who seldom allowed
> himself to be carried away by any feelings of poetic sensi-
> bility. . . . His tastes were . . . utilitarian.[38]

Among the few favorite novels of Thomas Jefferson noted by
Peden are *Don Quixote, The Vicar of Wakefield*. and Lawrence
Sterne's *A Sentimental Journey through France and Italy*.[39]

One may deduce from the relatively fewer holdings of fiction
in comparison to nonfiction and the fact that his holdings in
belles lettres were primarily classical that Jefferson was the
type of person who read for instruction and mental stimulation
rather than entertainment. This deduction is borne out by
Jefferson's own statements. On one occasion he called the contemporary novels a "mass of trash." He added:

> A great obstacle to good education is the inordinate
> passion prevalent for novels, and the time lost in that read-
> ing which should be instructively employed. When this
> poison infects the mind, . . . reason and fact, plain and
> unadorned, are rejected. . . . The result is a bloated imag-
> ination, sickly judgment, and disgust towards all the real
> businesses of life.[40]

Jefferson made an exception to his objection to fiction for those
works which teach a moral lesson:

> Some few, modeling their narratives, although fictitious,
> on the incidents of real life, have been able to make them
> interesting and useful vehicles of a sound morality. Such,

I think, are Marmontel's new moral tales, but not his old ones, which are really immoral. Such are the writings of Miss Edgeworth, and some of those of Madame Genlis.[41]

At a much earlier time in his life, Jefferson wrote more approvingly of the value of reading fiction:

The entertainments of fiction are useful as well as pleasant. That they are pleasant when well written every person feels who reads. But wherein is its utility, asks the reverend sage? I answer, everything is useful which contributes to fix in the principles and practices of virtue.[42]

It is significant that Jefferson found the chief value of reading fiction in the moral values such reading develops, especially when the fiction is based on truth and reality. He explained:

I appeal to every reader of feeling and sentiment whether the fictitious murder of Duncan by Macbeth in Shakespeare does not excite in him as great a horror of villany, as the real one of Henry IV by Ravaillac as related by Davila? . . . Thus a lively and lasting sense of filial duty is more effectually impressed on the mind of a son or daughter by reading King Lear, than by all the dry volumes of ethics, and divinity that were ever written. This is my idea of well written Romance, of Tragedy, Comedy and Epic poetry.[43]

Henry Randall notes that Jefferson also objected to the novels of Sir Walter Scott, passages of which his granddaughters read to him, because of Scott's exalting the feudal system and the chivalry of the Norman knights and nobility, whom Jefferson always referred to as "tyrants and robbers." It was the common Anglo-Saxon people that Jefferson admired.[44] On the whole, Jefferson abided by his own pronouncement for a library, "Nothing of mere amusement should lumber a public library."[45]

Jefferson's feelings about reading poetry were similar to those he held about reading novels. He enjoyed most the heroic epics of the classical writers and the Greek and English dramatists. In his youth he enjoyed and copied in his notebook passages from the English poets on beauty, nature, life, and love. Milton,

Shakespeare, Congreve, Mallet, and Ossian were some of his favorites.[46] Later in life Jefferson wrote:

> Of all men living I am the last who should undertake to decide as to the merits of poetry. In earlier life I was fond of it, and easily pleased. But as age and cares advanced the powers of fancy have declined.[47]

When he was criticizing too much novel reading, Jefferson also objected to poetry:

> For a like reason, too, much poetry should not be indulged. Some is useful for forming style and taste. Pope, Dryden, Thompson, Shakespeare, and of the French, Moliere, Racine, the Corneilles, may be read with pleasure and improvement.[48]

Jefferson had these favorites in his library.[49] He expressed something of the same thought in recommending to his nephew, Peter Carr, the most important works of poetry for study:

> In Greek and Latin poetry, you have read or will read at school, Virgil, Terence, Horace, Anacreon, Theocritus, Homer, Euripides, Sophocles. Read also Milton's "Paradise Lost," Shakespeare, Ossian, Pope's and Swift's works, in order to form your style in your own language.[50]

Jefferson had many editions of these favorite authors in his library.[51]

The many excerpts of favorite poetry which Jefferson copied in his commonplace book bear out the fact that he did enjoy poetry in his youth, at least. Chinard concludes from his study of these selections that "Jefferson's taste was the taste of his time," and that he enjoyed the "Romantic malady . . . [and] the pervasive melancholy of English poetry. . . . Poetry opened to him the portals of an enchanted world, and he even tried his hand at writing poems himself."[52]

It should be noted, however, that Jefferson was quite right in saying that imagination and fancy appealed to him less than thought and reason. His enjoyment of art tended to center on architecture rather than painting (see tables 1 and 2) and his interest in music turned to the mechanics of musical instruments and the mathematical structure of the scales rather than to the inspiration necessary to compose it or appreciate it.[53] Jefferson, similarly, was more interested in the rhythmical structure of poetry than the thought it conveyed. He wrote a long essay on poetry which dealt only with the subject of rhythm, stress, and pronunciation.[54]

Peden, who fails to note Jefferson's turning away from a youthful interest in romantic poetry and fiction in his mature concern for intellectual matters, is frequently confused and disappointed with Jefferson's traditional and utilitarian tastes.

> In general, Jefferson approved only of fiction which developed . . . the moral sense. . . .
> This is certainly not good criticism. . . . It is rather vicious utilitarianism which is likely to infect the roots of any creative endeavor.[55]

Peden does qualify his criticism of Jefferson's artistic interests by noting his occasional interest in works of imagination:

> If Jefferson's tastes were largely utilitarian, they were not completely so. In the fields of poetry, of the drama, and of fiction, he tended to emphasize the importance and value of works which fostered the moral sense rather than those which pleased or stimulated the artistic and aesthetic. As a result, his critical judgments were not always the best. On the other hand, he was neither devoid of imagination nor incapable of reacting to poetic stimuli.[56]

Peden is making a value judgment which is open to challenge in placing the artistic sense above the moral one. This writer, for one, would side with Jefferson as to which sensibility is more important to society, for it seems that Jefferson is correct in maintaining that great art and literature do strike a deep moral tone.

Although Jefferson outgrew his youthful enthusiasm for English romantic poetry, he found more to understand and appreciate in the great classical dramatists and poets with increasing age and experience of human living. He became more critical and more discriminating in his judgment, but he continued to value the great classics, Lehmann argues, for two reasons:

> He continued enthusiastically to read Greek and Latin poetry. Poetry . . . was the realm of pure beauty. It offered a natural experience to man, who was endowed with an innate sense of beauty. . . .
> Knowledge of the human heart was the true province of that great branch of the tree of imagination, poetry. . . .
> The epic enlargement of Homer, Virgil, Dante, and Milton . . . , [especially] Homer and his monumental rendering of human nature, became to him the essence of poetical imagination.[57]

In his essay on poetry Jefferson wrote:

> When young any composition pleases which unites a little sense, some imagination, and some rhythm, in doses however small. But as we advance in life these things fall off one by one, and I suspect we are left at last with only Homer and Virgil, perhaps with Homer alone. He, like "Hope, travels on nor quits us when we die."[58]

Such proved to be Jefferson's own experience. One of his grandchildren wrote to Randall:

> In his youth he had loved poetry, but by the time I was old enough to observe, he had lost his taste for it, except for Homer and the great Athenian tragics, which he continued to the last to enjoy. He went over the works of Eschylus, Sophocles and Euripides, not very long before . . . his death.[59]

Lehmann explains Jefferson's enthusiasm for classical literature in this way:

> Jefferson was a decided Hellenist in his admiration for language and in his literary tastes. . . . The vigor of pas-

[89]

sion, the awe-inspiring grandeur of epos and tragedy, the copiousness of the richest language, its . . . forceful expression, breath-taking spell of diction and haunting beauty of euphonious sound—these were the fruits he gathered from the tree of Greek imagination.[60]

In his study of Jefferson's libraries, Peden placed religion next among Jefferson's interests. Peden counted some 200 works on religion in Jefferson's largest library, and 47 in his last library, with 180 listed for the University of Virginia Library. In the collections, Peden noticed many copies of the Bible in different languages and many copies of the New Testament, as well as a copy of the Koran. Among tne authors chosen were St. Thomas Aquinas, Bede, Calvin, Martin Luther, Jeremy Taylor's *Works*, and Priestley's *Corruptions of Christianity*.[61]

The last field of interest discussed by Peden as shown by the Jeffersonian libraries is that of science, which, taken in its broadest sense, had the most titles of all classifications, 800 in Jefferson's main library and 1,000 in the more specialized library for the university. The subjects covered were "mathematics, natural history, natural philosophy, agriculture, horticulture, botany, zoology, mineralogy, geology, chemistry, medicine, physiology, architecture, music, rhetoric, and the like."[62]

The indication of Jefferson's keen interest in science, despite his liberal arts educational background and his lifelong preoccupation with the law and politics, is supported by evidence from his writings and his activities. Scholars have noted his respect for the scientific method and his own orderly nature, as reflected in his daily meteorological recordings and his detailed farm book records.[63] He advised the young men whose education he guided to pursue studies in science as well as the classics.[64]

One reason for Jefferson's interest in science was the practical need to improve the agricultural yield of his plantation and to find the best means of carrying on the building work at Monticello. He drew up detailed plans and drawings for each of his fields, allotting so many workers, so many animals, so much seed, and so many tools to each field according to a seven-year rotation of crops. Unfortunately the weather and human activities did not often produce the expected results. Jefferson also put his efficient engineer's mind to work on building improvements, recording detailed figures on how long it took "Ford's [slave] Phil . . . to dig and carry to a distance of 50 yds., 5 cubical yds. of earth . . . [in] his barrow. . . . "[65] Isaac Jefferson reminisced about building at Monticello:

> Isaac remembers John Nelson, an Englishman at work at Monticello: he was an inside worker, a finisher. The blacksmith was Billy Ore; the carriage-maker Davy Watson. . . . Monticello-house was pulled down in part and built up again some six or seven times. One time it was struck by lightning. It had a Franklin rod at one end. Old Master used to say, "If it hadn't been for that Franklin the whole house would have gone." They was forty years at work upon that house before Mr. Jefferson stopped building.[66]

Jefferson had something of Ben Franklin's interest in inventions, especially to make life easier at Monticello. Isaac remembered Jefferson's "copyin machine" to make a duplicate copy of a handwritten letter or document and the "dumb-waiter" that would bring up "water or fruit" to the library at the turn of a crank.[67] In discussing science with his friend Thomas Cooper, Jefferson wrote:

> You know the just esteem which attached itself to Dr. Franklin's science, because he always endeavored to direct it to something useful in private life. The chemists have not been attentive enough to this. I have wished to see their science applied to domestic objects, to malting, for instance, brewing, making cider, to fermentation and distillation generally, to the making of bread, butter, cheese, soap, to the incubation of eggs, etc.[68]

Jefferson thus anticipated the modern use of applied science and research in industry.

Jefferson made some important contributions to agriculture by his use of applied science. By applying uniform mathematical rules he developed a new plow to use at Monticello which attracted attention in France and from the English Board of Trade.[69]

Constantly seeking to learn new methods and crops to culti-
vate, Jefferson was observant of European agriculture during
his travels abroad and brought back new seeds to try. Early in
his life he encouraged Philip Mazzei in his efforts to establish
the cultivation of Italian grapes, vegetables, and citrus fruits
on land adjoining Monticello.[70] A more successful and lasting
effort of Jefferson to improve agriculture in America, which
he listed as one of his services to his countrymen, was the introduction of "heavy upland rice . . . [into] South Carolina and
Georgia" and making the Rivanna River navigable.[71]

Jefferson was equally interested in the theoretical side of
science, particularly its philosophical implications. Like the
other Enlightenment thinkers, Jefferson revered the work of
Newton, Locke, and Bacon. As man learned more and more to
understand and follow the laws of God's creation he would
make more and more progress in understanding and controlling
the world of nature, in freeing his social and political institutions from tyranny and exploitation, and in understanding and
using his own reason and enlightened thought.[72] Science and
progress would lead men to a new stage of freedom and happiness. Jefferson articulated his Enlightenment faith in science
near the end of his life in these words:

> When I contemplate the immense advances in science and
> discoveries in the arts which have been made within the
> period of my life, I look forward with confidence to equal
> advances by the present generation, and have no doubt
> they will consequently be as much wiser than we have been
> as we than our fathers were, and they than the burners of
> witches.[73]

For Jefferson and the men of the Enlightenment, progress of
the physical sciences implied progress of the social sciences
and vice versa. Material progress meant less poverty, and freedom of thought for scientific pursuits would aid in overcoming
ignorance and superstition, they felt. In Europe, particularly,
the Enlightenment became an intellectual and religious struggle
for men's minds and for political power.

Jefferson's interest in science, so clearly reflected in his library
holdings, was, then, both practical and philosophical. Like

Franklin, he was honored by many scientific societies in America
and Europe, and he did much through his own studies and
influence to advance the cause of science in his time.[74]

Scholars who have studied Jefferson's intellectual life have
been impressed as Peden is by his "active mind, . . . deep and
profound . . . storehouse of information, and indefatigable
diligence.[75] Although Jefferson was not willing to become
a specialist in any one field, he studied deeply enough to make
important contributions in the fields of architecture, education,
political science, natural science, history, literature, and, not
the least important, library science. In at least two scholarly
fields of study, philology and Americana, he was an expert
and an innovator, according to Peden.[76] Jefferson was, in fact,
one of the last and most famous of the eighteenth-century
generalists or philosophers. Peden, commenting on the wide
interests shown by Jefferson's library, writes of Jefferson:

> In his interest in history, religion, law, and the like he was
> following . . . the pattern of the average eighteenth
> century Virginia gentleman of substance and position,
> although on a much grander scale.[77]

Library of Congress's Analysis of Jefferson's Library

An analysis of the emphasis of Jefferson's main library which
he sold to Congress, based on the more detailed and thorough
study of Sowerby,[78] which was produced as part of the Bicentenniel honoring of Jefferson's birth in 1943 when the Jefferson
Memorial was built in Washington,[79] reveals similar conclusions to those drawn by Peden in his analysis of Jefferson's
several libraries, although the title counts are not the same.
It is often difficult to determine which modern subject classification corresponds to the subjects of Jefferson's time, as for
example, "Law of Nature." Different scholars may count the
same work under "History," "Law," "Philosophy," or "Ethics."
The title count of the works in Jefferson's library under each
subject as he classified them, based on his catalog entry numbers
as verified and cumulatively counted by Sowerby, is given in
table 3.

When the titles from Jefferson's library are grouped and

TABLE 3
SUBJECT ANALYSIS OF THOMAS JEFFERSON'S LIBRARY
ACCORDING TO HIS OWN CLASSIFICATION

CHAPTER NUMBER	CHAPTER HEADING	NUMBER OF TITLES
1	Ancient History	154
2	Modern History—Foreign	208
3	Modern History—British	143
4	Modern History—American	91
	—Newspapers	73
5	Ecclesiastical History	25
6	Natural Philosophy	36
7	Agriculture	84
8	Chemistry	30
9	Surgery	7
10	Medicine	102
11	Anatomy	11
12	Zoology	48
13	Botany	36
14	Mineralogy	6
15	Technical Arts	143
16	Ethics—Moral Philosophy	138
	—Law of Nature & Nations	89
17	Religion	281
18	Equity	43
19	Common Law	228
20	Law—Merchant	10
21	Law—Maritime	17
22	Law—Ecclesiastical	19
23	Foreign Law	76
24	Politics	1,336
	(Classed under Ancient, Modern, Special Governments: France, Monarchical, Revolutionary, Imperial; England, Colonies, Constitution, Parliament, Dependancies; United States, Colonial, Revolutionary, Reconstituted; States; Political oeconomy—Statistics, Commerce, Finances. Many are pamphlets bound together in one volume.)	
25	Mathematics—Pure—Arithmetic	38
26	Mathematics—Pure—Geometry	23
27	Physico—Mathematics	64
	(Classed under Mechanics, Statics, Dynamics, Pneumatics, Phonics, Optics)	
28	Astronomy	37
29	Geography (Many are maps)—	
	General	27
	Europe	66
	Asia	30
	Africa	14
	America	191
30	Architecture	43
31	Gardening, Painting, Sculpture	25
32	Music	11
33	Poetry—Epic	44
34	Romance, Tales—Fables	77
35	Pastorals, Odes, Elegies	75
36	Didactic	77

Table 3—Continued

CHAPTER NUMBER	CHAPTER HEADING	NUMBER OF TITLES
37	Tragedy	32
38	Comedy	32
39	Dialogue—Epistolary	32
40	Logic—Rhetoric—Orations	47
41	Criticism, Theory	18
42	Criticism, Bibliography	25
43	Criticism, Language	167
	(Classed under General, Polyglot, Oriental, Greek, Latin, Italian, Spanish, French, Northern, English, Welsh)	
44	Polygraphical	46
	(General works, encyclopedias, reference works, etc.)	

SOURCE: Sowerby, *Catalogue*, 1: 1-554, 2: 1-429, 3: 1-477, 4: 1-562, 5: 1-184.

totaled according to modern subject headings, the subject having the most titles, 1,336, is "Government and Politics." Many of these titles, however, were small pamphlets or bound collections of articles filed by Jefferson. Another subject with a large number of titles was Jefferson's profession of "Law," which had 692 titles in its many branches of classifications.

For "Religion," on the other hand, or "Theology," Jefferson had only 271 titles. He listed another 216 titles under subjects that would fall under "Philosophy" today (excluding those titles he listed under branches of philosophy which are now considered to be under "Law," "Politics," "Social Science," or "Science"). He also had many titles under "Ecclesiastical Law" and "Ecclesiastical History" which should be considered in connection with religion.

It can be seen at once, then, that Jefferson's library does very much reflect his professional interests. Jefferson himself commented on his library to Librarian Watterston:

Thus the law having been my profession, and politics the occupation to which . . . the times in which I lived called my particular attention, my provision of books in these lines, and in those most nearly connected with them was more copious . . . [than those of] a physician or theologist.[80]

The second largest number of titles in Jefferson's library fell under the classification of "Science," ranging all the way from Euclid's geometry in the original Greek to how to treat a sick horse. There were 710 titles under Jefferson's several classifications for types of mathematics, mechanics, and sciences. This result supports Peden's finding of a strong emphasis upon science and is documented by Jefferson's many writings and activities which indicate his Enlightenment interest in science, his frontiersman's curiosity about nature, and his plantation owner's concern with agriculture. Jefferson wrote:

> I am for encouraging the progress of science in all its branches; and not for raising a hue and cry against the sacred name of philosophy; [nor] for awing the human mind . . . to a distrust of its own vision . . . to go backwards instead of forwards to look for improvement.[81]

Jefferson had the Enlightenment belief in science and progress which amounted almost to a religion, and his library reflects this conviction.

The third subject of interest for Jefferson as measured by the number of titles in his library was "History" which had 627 titles in its various branches, ranging from ancient Greek classics and accounts of early settlements in America to histories of events in which Jefferson took part. Jefferson explained this emphasis upon politics, science, and history in his library when he wrote to Samuel Smith, chairman of the Library Committee of Congress, recommending the purchase of his library for Congress. He had made a special effort, Jefferson wrote, while he resided abroad to collect "everything which related to America, and indeed whatever was rare and valuable in every science" from all the "principal book-marts." Jefferson concluded:

> After my return to America, I was led to procure, also, whatever related to the duties of those in the high concerns of the nation. So that the collection, . . . while it includes what is valuable in science and literature generally, extends more particularly to whatever belongs to the American statesman. In the diplomatic and parliamentary branches, it is particularly full.[82]

Jefferson was quite correct in mentioning his valuable collection of literature, for he had 602 titles that could be classified under "Literature and Language," making this the next largest classification in his library. The size of Jefferson's collection of ancient classics and the preponderance of good literature over light, amusing literature is noteworthy, as well as Jefferson's subdividing his collection into many types of literature (see table 3). Jefferson's interest in the grammar, etymology, and philology of different languages, is reflected in his holdings. Jefferson had a special interest in primitive languages and did much research on the Anglo-Saxon and American Indian languages. Hoping to study relationships with European and Asian vocabularies, he collected Indian vocabularies.[83] He wrote a technical discussion on the Anglo-Saxon language for the University of Virginia[84] and collected his addresses to the Indian tribes.[85]

Jefferson not only had many works on grammar and many dictionaries in various languages but he had many other reference works treating diversified subjects which he classified as "Polygraphical" or "Miscellaneous." He had 71 such encyclopedias and reference works. Many of the works in his collection on "Geography," which numbered 328 titles, were maps and reference works also. This fondness for useful reference works reflected Jefferson's desire as a librarian to have the tools necessary to provide whatever information might be desired by those turning to his library collection for help.

The section on fine arts was the smallest section of all in Jefferson's library, numbering 79 titles. It reflected Jefferson's particular artistic interests of architecture, gardening, sculpture, and music, with a few works on painting (see table 3).

On the whole, from the study of Jefferson's library collection and from the comments of Jefferson himself about his reading interests, one has the impression of a large, well-balanced, carefully chosen library that would provide basic education in all fields and specialized knowledge for Jefferson's professional fields of law and government. The library was well deserving of its creator's recommendation as "the best chosen collection of its size probably in America, containing a great mass of what is most rare and valuable, and especially of what relates to America."[86]

Comparison with the Library of John Adams

How does Jefferson's library compare with the libraries of other men of his time? Did other founding fathers share his interest in law and the theory of government? Did his contemporaries share his enthusiasm for history, science, and the ancient classics or was Jefferson unique? For example, it would be interesting to compare Jefferson's library with that of his friendly rival from New England, John Adams.

Unfortunately, the record of Adams's library holdings has not been as well preserved as that of Jefferson's. Upon Adams's death most of his library was incorporated into that of his son, John Quincy Adams, as their different bookplates make clear, but part of John Adams' library was presented by him to the town of Quincy. It was not until 1893 that the whole library was reunited and found a safe and lasting place in the Boston Public Library.[87]

For purposes of comparison, the number of titles in both Jefferson's and Adams's libraries are given by modern subject classifications in table 4. Since the number of works from Adams's library that have been preserved is so small, percentages are also given for each classification from both libraries.

Some interesting facts emerge from these admittedly imperfect data comparing the reading interests of Adams and Jefferson. Both men, as might be expected, share a large interest in history, government and politics, and law, although Adams had only six percent of his collection classified under "Law" compared with fourteen percent for Jefferson. It may be that less of Adams's lawbooks survived as being still useful. Both libraries show about the same emphasis upon geography and travel and upon reference works.

There also is a similar emphasis upon literature, although the presence of so many works classed as "Fiction" and "Biography" in Adams's library, lacking in Jefferson's classification, in contrast to Jefferson's works on grammar, language, and philology listed under "Literature," which are lacking in Adams' library, may indicate a greater interest in works of imagination on the part of Adams. The extensive correspondence between the two friends reveals that Adams humorously proposed the "frivolous" imaginative question "Would you

TABLE 4
SUBJECT ANALYSIS OF JEFFERSON'S AND ADAMS'S LIBRARIES

SUBJECT	JEFFERSON'S LIBRARY		ADAMS'S LIBRARY	
	Number of Titles	Percentage	Number of Titles	Percentage
Government and Politics	1,336	27	38	17
Law	692	14	19	6
History	627	13	68	24
Science	710	14	11	4
Geography	328	7	18	6
Theology	271	6	26	9
Philosophy	216	4	20	7
Literature and Language	602	12	32	10
Fiction	0	0	8	3
Biography (Not so classed by Jefferson. Often classed with history in early libraries.)	0	0	20	7
Miscellaneous (Reference)	71	2	13	4
Arts	79	2	2	1
Commerce (Social Science) (Not so classed by Jefferson.)	0	0	5	2

SOURCE: For Jefferson's library see Sowerby, *Catalogue*, 1:1-554, 2:1-429, 3:1-477, 4:1-562, 5:1-184. For Adams's library see Henry Adams, *A Catalogue of the Books of John Quincy Adams Deposited in the Boston Athenaeum* (Boston: Athenaeum, 1938) pp. 79-132.

go back to your Cradle and live over again Your 70 Years?"[88] provoking from the more serious and literary Jefferson the answer:

> I say Yea. I think with you that it is a good world on the whole, that it has been framed on a principle of benevolence, and more pleasure than pain dealt out to us. . . . I steer my bark with Hope in the head, leaving Fear astern.[89]

On the other hand, the classification of Adams's works under "Fiction" and "Biography" may simply be due to Adams's library being classified at a later date when those classifications had come into use. Such is clearly the case for the heading "Social Science" which Jefferson did not use, although he was

[99]

one of the world's most important writers and thinkers on the theory of government and society.[90]

Both Adams and Jefferson had a similar classical education and shared an interest in the great classical works of literature, as their discussions of poetry and their fondness for exchanging Latin and Greek quotations indicates.[91] Jefferson clearly sustained his interest in the original classical works more than Adams did, for Adams replied to Jefferson's Greek quotations humorously:

> Lord! Lord! What can I do, with so much Greek? When I was of your Age, young Man, i.e. 7 or 8 or 9 Years ago I felt, a kind of pang of Affection, for one of the flames of my Youth, and again paid my Addresses to Isocrates and Dionissius. . . . I collected all my Lexicons and Grammers . . . but I found, that if I looked a Word to-day, in less than a Week I had to look it again. It was to little better purpose, than writing Letters on a pail of Water.[92]

Both Jefferson and Adams had a low percentage of works on art in their libraries, although Jefferson's interest in music, architecture, and sculpture seems to have been greater than Adams's. One striking difference reflected in these library collections is the much greater interest in science on the part of Jefferson. Science ranks second in his reading interests, comprising fourteen percent of the whole library, while it is near the bottom of Adams's interests, comprising only four percent of the total (see table 4). It is clear that Jefferson's interest in mechanics and invention and his hope of progress for mankind from applications of the scientific method was an attitude he shared more with Benjamin Franklin than with John Adams. Adams's mind ran more to speculation and philosophy and Jefferson's mind more to particular details, as indicated by the larger proportion of Adams's library classed as "Philosophy": seven percent as compared with four percent. Cappon summarizes the difference:

> Adams's mind ran to moral philosophy rather than natural philosophy—the social sciences and ideology rather than to the natural sciences. . . . Adams was a more profound

thinker than Jefferson, more intrigued by the abstract proposition. . . . Jefferson, the practical philosopher . . . of the Enlightenment, strove always to put things to work, having [once] grasped the principle.[93]

One difference of interests shown by the comparison of the libraries of Adams and Jefferson does deserve investigation— that of religion. The reader will note that sixteen percent of the Adams library falls in the categories of theology and philosophy compared with ten percent for Jefferson's library (see table 4). Is this a significant difference? Is it evidence that Adams, coming from Puritan New England, was more religious and conservative while Jefferson, reared in Cavalier Virginia, was broader in his interests and more of a freethinker?

It makes a tempting generalization to hold that the early religious character of the New England colonies and the strong leadership exerted by its clergy did shape its people into a more conservative and religious mold than in Virginia, which was settled by more of the courtier class with freer morals and more cultivated tastes, and which followed the less strict Anglican church.

Such an able historian of New England as James Truslow Adams has argued that, while the New England leaders were well educated and early fostered common-school education, they were more preoccupied with religion and Calvinism than the more cultivated Virginia settlers.[94] Samuel Elliott Morrison takes issue with this common assessment of Puritan life in general and with Adams' study in particular.[95]

Morrison admits the strong theological and puritanical nature of New England culture, but cites considerable evidence from New England educational curricula indicating that Puritanism, as it flourished in New England, had far more intellectual, classical, and humanist content than most people have realized.[96] He comments:

The humanist tradition . . . went hand in hand with conquering Puritanism into the clearings of New England. The glory that was Greece shown down a path that the Roman legions had never traced; and "light-foote Nymphs" played hide-and-seek in college yard with homespun lads who would pass the remainder of their days ministering to rural communities.[97]

Thomas Keys, in a study of the colonial libraries of New England and the South made in 1934, believes he detects a greater interest in theology among the separatist Puritans and a greater interest in the latest English literary tastes among the Virginia Cavaliers. But he notes exceptions.[98] Peden argues that the average Virginia library showed a broader and more literary interest than the New England ones.[99]

To the present writer it seems that, while there is some basis for the popular generalizations about Puritan New England and Cavalier Virginia put forward by articles such as those cited by James Truslow Adams, the more careful studies of Philip Alexander Bruce and Samuel Morrison are more convincing. Certainly different historical background and differences in social and economic conditions greatly affected the development of the people of New England and Virginia. It is all too easy, however, to exaggerate these differences of region and neglect individual differences. Consider William Byrd, who, far more of a pleasure-loving Cavalier than Thomas Jefferson, wrote in his diary of kissing a friend's wife on the bed and of then piously begging pardon of God in his prayers that night.[100] The truth is always more complex than easy generalizations allow.

If John Adams and Thomas Jefferson are taken as representatives of the best of both regions, one finds both men equally moral or puritanical in their personal lives, although Jefferson was more tolerant and understanding than Adams.[101] It is true that Adams boasted of having read more titles in theology than Jefferson had ever seen,[102] but Jefferson replied by citing his own reading in religion.[103]

It is evident that Jefferson, like most librarians, selected the works he found useful and ignored the ones he found uninteresting. He was in religion, as in other subjects that intrigued his probing mind, a thorough scholar of the aspects he wished to study.[104] It would be as false to say he was uninterested in religion as it would be to say that Adams had no intellectual interests beyond religion. The most that can be determined from the larger percentage of philosophy in Adams's library than in Jefferson's is that Jefferson's interest in religion was of a more practical and less speculative nature than Adams's. This conclusion is verified by the writings of the two men.[105]

Comparison with Other Contemporary Libraries

How do Jefferson's library and reading interests compare with those of his friends of the Virginia aristocracy? Were Jefferson's interests the same or was he unique? Were the Virginian Cavaliers as intellectual as Peden declared or more given to gambling and fox hunting, as Jefferson complained?[106] It is enlightening to compare Jefferson's library with that of another Virginia planter and aristocratic bibliophile of only a slightly earlier period, William Byrd. Elmer Johnson describes Byrd's library as follows:

> In the South, the largest private library of the later colonial period was that of William Byrd II of Westover, Virginia. Byrd's father had built up a large estate and had started to collect books, but it was the son who, before his death in 1740, enlarged the library to nearly four thousand volumes. Byrd was a planter, lawyer and public official, as well as a writer, and his library reflected the cultural level and interests of the well-to-do planter. Almost a fourth of the collection was made up of works of history, with another fourth in classical literature, and about ten percent each in English literature, law, and science. There were a number of volumes in French and Latin, and theology was represented by a few works of the church fathers, some volumes on the Church of England, and some current books of sermons.[107]

Thomas Keys, in his study of American colonial libraries, made a summary of the Byrd library based on material provided by John Spencer Bassett, which is given in table 5. By comparing this information of Byrd's library with that of Jefferson's library in table 4, it can be seen that the two Virginians had a similar interest in history and in classical literature, and a common interest in French writings. Byrd had more light literature, and it is clear from the writings of both men that Jefferson was a more profound thinker and serious scholar. Jefferson showed

TABLE 5
SUBJECT ANALYSIS OF THE BYRD LIBRARY

SUBJECT	NUMBER OF TITLES	PERCENTAGE
Theology	233	11.5
History	458	22.5
Science	147	7.5
Law	226	12
Medicine	143	7.5
Literature		
Classical	394	19.5
Foreign (chiefly French)	46	2.5
English	176	8
Reference	44	2
Social Science	41	2
Arts	16	.5
School	66	2
Superstition	14	.5
Unclassified	44	2

SOURCE: William Byrd, *The Writings of Colonel William Byrd in Virginia*, ed. John Spencer Bassett (New York: Doubleday Page and Co., 1901), Appendix A; Keys, "Libraries of the Colonies," p. 59.

more of an interest in the study of law, government, and politics, and much more of an interest in science. Both libraries have a similar amount of religion and philosophy, eleven percent. Byrd has even less of an interest in the fine arts than Jefferson. The presence of a considerable number of books for school purposes in Byrd's library may be due to the fact that he employed a tutor for his children at home who classified the library to make it useful in teaching his charges.[108]   The classification of "Superstition" most likely represented a special interest.

It would be most enlightening if we could compare Jefferson's reading interests with those of his like-minded contemporary, Benjamin Franklin, but it is difficult to make such a comparison. Johnson points out:

Benjamin Franklin also had a notable private library of his own, in addition to his activities in connection with other libraries. He bought books frequently on his trips to Europe, usually books that he wanted to read or use. At the time of his death in 1780, Franklin owned more than four thousand volumes, including a wide range of topics.

Willed to his grandsons, Franklin's books were scattered, with many of them coming on the market in 1801, when they were sold by a Philadelphia bookseller. Fortunately, many of Franklin's volumes were recognizable as such, and about a thousand of them can now be located in various libraries.[109]

With a bit of luck Franklin's library might have been preserved along side of Jefferson's library in the Library of Congress, for the Philadelphia bookseller entrusted with the sale of Franklin's library was agent for Jefferson. He appealed to Jefferson to get Congress to buy Franklin's library. Jefferson consulted with the chairman of the library committee, Abraham Baldwin, but had to inform the bookseller that the committee lacked the money to buy Franklin's library "in part or in toto."[110]
to
Although we do not have the record of Franklin's own library, we do have a record of the Philadelphia Company Library, the early subscription library which Franklin did so much to organize. Edwin Wolf has done a detailed analysis of this library. His results are summarized in table 6.

Assuming that the Philadelphia Company Library does reflect Franklin's interests and tastes, it indicates that both Franklin and Jefferson had strong interests in science and in history (compare tables 4 and 6). Franklin's circulating library lacked Jefferson's preponderant interest in law, government, and politics, having only a few such works classed with "Social

TABLE 6
SUBJECT ANALYSIS OF FRANKLIN'S
PHILADELPHIA CO. LIBRARY

SUBJECT	NUMBER OF TITLES	PERCENTAGE
History	91	34
Literature	55	20
Science	51	19
Theology	25	9
Philosophy	28	10
Social Sciences	21	8

SOURCE: Edwin Wolf, "Franklin and His Friends Choose Their Books," *An American Library History Reader*, ed. by John David Marshall (Hamden, Conn.: Shoe String Press, 1961) p. 21.

Sciences." This difference is understandable in view of the fact that Franklin was not a lawyer and the Philadelphia library was intended for the general public. Possibly Franklin's personal library would show more works for the statesman. Both libraries show a high interest in literature, but Franklin's library lacked the emphasis upon Greek and Latin classics and works in foreign languages. A popular library would be expected to contain few works in other languages, but this lack in Franklin's library does point to a significant difference in the education and interests of the two men, a cultural difference that is reinforced by the lack of any works on the "Fine Arts" in Franklin's library. Franklin's library does contain nineteen percent "Theology and Philosophy" compared with ten percent for Jefferson's, a fact which is somewhat surprising, considering the popular nature of Franklin's library. This difference tends to emphasize the lack of interest on the part of Jefferson in speculative works of philosophy which the comparison of his library with that of John Adams also showed. Wolf points out that few theological tracts or books of sermons are to be found in the Philadelphia library, although publisher's records indicate many such works were being printed in Philadelphia. He concludes:

> Hence, it may be assumed that the Philadelphians who wanted a regular fare of sermons and religious polemics found them easily and cheaply available at every bookstore. They sent abroad for more expensive works not printed here.[111]

The question arises whether Jefferson's library interests were more cultivated than popular interests and whether Franklin's Philadelphia Company Library had different interests than other social libraries for the public. Table 7 indicates the holdings of some other popular libraries.

A comparison of these libraries with Franklin's library in Philadelphia (see table 5) and with Jefferson's library (see table 4) indicates a similar emphasis upon history and literature, although the social libraries show a much greater interest in light literature and fiction, which Jefferson disdained and Franklin lacked. These popular libraries reflect a considerable interest in "Geography and Travel" ranging from nine to seventeen percent in contrast to Jefferson's seven percent (see table 4).

TABLE 7
SUBJECT ANALYSIS OF SOCIAL LIBRARIES, BY PERCENTAGE

SUBJECT	Farmington, Connecticut 1785	Brookfield, Vermont 1791	Mechanic's, New Haven, 1793	Guild, Boston, 1788
Theology, religion	22	28	9	7
History, biography	27	29	25	19
Literature	28	9	20	20
Geography, travel	10	11	17	9
Science			1	3
Fiction	5	12	22	33
Miscellaneous (law, politics, periodicals, reference, unidentified)	8	11	6	3
Social Sciences				1
Text books and juvenile books				5

SOURCE: Jesse H. Shera, *Foundations of the Public Library: the Origins of the Public Library Movement in New England, 1629-1855* (Hamden, Connecticut: Shoe String Press, 1965) pp. 103, 149.

The Farmington and Brookfield libraries agree with the Philadelphia company library in having a much larger percentage of their holdings in religion and philosophy than Jefferson had, but the Mechanic's and Guild libraries had less in religion than Jefferson did. The social libraries had very little interest in science in contrast to the high interest of Jefferson and Franklin. These libraries agreed with the Philadelphia library in having few works on fine arts or languages, in contrast to the number of such works in Jefferson's, reflecting his cultivated interests. They also agreed with the Franklin library in their lack of holdings in law, government, and politics in which Jefferson had specialized. The Mechanic's library had a special interest in technical books and the Guild library in school books similar to the Byrd library's interest in school books (compare with table 5).

These findings indicate that Jefferson was more highly educated and cultivated in his tastes in reading than the general public, especially in the areas of his scholarly interests. How do his library holdings and interests compare with those of college libraries designed for people of his same educational level and interests? Did Jefferson share the interests of educated people of his time or did he have special interests? The library holdings of four early American colleges, based on their early published catalogs and book lists, are given in table 8.

TABLE 8

SUBJECT ANALYSIS OF EARLY AMERICAN COLLEGE LIBRARIES

Subject	WILLIAM AND MARY, 1695		HARVARD, 1790		YALE, 1791		COLLEGE of RHODE ISLAND (Brown), 1798	
	Number of Titles	Percentage	Number of Titles	Percentage	Number of Titles	Percentage	Number of Titles	Percentage
Theology	66	42	4,520	49	852	56	420	34
Philosophy	2	1	284	3	71	4	48	4
Literature	10	6	974	10	175	11	202	17
History	27	17	1,144	12	183	12	141	12
Biography	5	3	216	2	16	1	42	3
Science	12	8	813	9	179	11	126	10
Geography	6	4	210	2	33	2	45	4
Government	8	5	397	4	13	1	25	2
Law	7	4	204	2	23	1	20	2
Commerce (Social Science)	5	3	97	1	5	a	15	1
Arts	2	1	136	1	7	a	15	1
Miscellaneous	3	2	259	3	21	1	33	3
Unclassified	5	3	42	a	4	a	88	7

SOURCE: Joe Walker Krause, "Book Collections of Five Colonial College Libraries: a Subject Analysis" (unpublished Ph.D. dissertation, University of Illinois, 1960), pp. 109, 196, 179, 184.

a Less than one percent.

It is unfortunate that Krause could not find later information to use for William and Mary College since its list is nearly one hundred years earlier than the other colleges. The percentage figures for the largest holdings by classifications do not materially differ from the other college holdings, however, perhaps indicating that the academic world changes rather slowly. The most noticeable thing about all the college holdings is the very large amount of theology, ranging from thirty-four to fifty-six percent, much greater than Jefferson's, Adams's, Franklin's, or any of the social libraries. Harvard alone had 4,520 theological works! This religious emphasis clearly reflects the fact that all of these colleges were related to the church of their colony and were intended to educate clergy for the churches, even though no other institutions of higher education were then available. Nearly all early American colleges were church established, which points up the need Jefferson felt to create a liberal, non-sectarian university in Virginia. Contrasting with the high percentage of theological works is the small percentage of works on philosophy, three or four percent. The church authorities apparently did not wish to disturb the ministerial students with upsetting works of speculation.

The colleges' interest in history is essentially the same as that shown by Jefferson's library (compare tables 8 and 4), in the twelve percent range. The circulating libraries, in contrast, had a larger percentage of their collections in history, twenty to thirty percent (see tables 6 and 7). They also had more in geography and travel, perhaps because such needed reference works made up a larger percentage of their smaller collections.

Jefferson's holdings in literature correspond almost exactly to that of the colleges, twelve percent. The colleges, like Jefferson, lack the fiction class and stress the classics and good literature of which Jefferson was so fond. This evidence indicates Jefferson acquired his taste for classical reading at college. He continued to expand his classical knowledge during a lifetime of reading. His commonplace book, with its many quotations of classic literature, documents his college interest in good literature.[112]

The colleges pretty much agree in their holdings on science, about ten percent, as compared with the popular libraries which had very little science. The colleges do not show as much interest in science as Jefferson and Franklin do in their libraries. This finding is supported by the many scientific activities and writings by Jefferson and Franklin, indicating they were both ahead of their time in their scientific studies and understandings. The colleges all had about one percent of their holdings classified as "Art." This interest represents a greater cultural interest than the social libraries but it is less than the two percent of Jefferson's extensive collection. Jefferson's interest in foreign languages and in adapting agriculture, architecture, and culture from abroad to the American scene, which he acquired from his travels and reading, was clearly in advance of his American contemporaries.

Concerning the subjects of "Law, Government, and Politics," the college libraries had more holdings than the social libraries but still had only from two to nine percent while Jefferson's library had forty-one percent. It may be significant that William and Mary College had more of its library in law than the other colleges, perhaps indicating an interest on the part of Virginia's youth to train for the law as Jefferson did.

It is very evident that none of the libraries studied could match Jefferson's for the scope, variety, and depth of its holdings not only in law, but in government and political and social science. He had indeed, as he wrote, put together a collection of what was most "rare and valuable" not only for "science, . . . literature," and history "related to America," which were Jefferson's special interests, but of law and government and "whatever belongs to the American statesman" that was unmatched by any library in America.[113] It is noteworthy that, of all the libraries studied in this comparison, only the Harvard library was comparable to Jefferson's in size and nearly half of Harvard's library was in theology. With the exceptions of theological disputations, which Jefferson purposely avoided, and fictional literature, of which he disapproved, Jefferson's library was probably superior to any other in the country at that time in nearly all subject classifications.

Summary and Conclusions

A close study of Jefferson's library gives valuable indications of his main interests, important convictions, and chief traits of character, since reading and discussing books and the collection and care of his library were some of Jefferson's chief interests from his early college days until his death. Various scholars have noted important interests of Jefferson reflected in his library. Cousins noted Jefferson's broad interest in liberal arts subjects,[114] Koch studied Jefferson's interest in the philosophy of government and of man,[115] Boorstin emphasized Jefferson's emphasis on the philosophy of nature,[116] and Lehmann has pointed out the strong influence, seen both in Jefferson's library and in his study interests, of Greek and Roman classical writings.[117]

Comparative studies of the contents of Jefferson's libraries based on the researches of Peden, on the several libraries which Jefferson selected, and on the detailed catalog compiled by Sowerby, of Jefferson's main library which he sold to Congress, support the findings of scholars concerning Jefferson's extensive literary interests, but add important insights concerning the relative importance of Jefferson's varied interests based on the comparative size of the different sections of his libraries. Although statistical details vary in small degrees, these studies largely agree concerning Jefferson's main literary interests and are supported by Jefferson's own statements of his chief interests and beliefs.

Since, as Jefferson commented, the law was his profession and politics the occupation to which the times called him, "Government and Politics" and "Law" comprised the largest sections in his library,[118] being twenty-seven and fourteen percent respectively (see table 4). An examination of the titles in these sections indicates that, although he had a full collection of technical law books on many branches of law and many collected pamphlets and articles on partisan politics, Jefferson's chief interest lay in works concerning the philosophy of government and society. He was chiefly concerned with matters now discussed under the subjects of political and social science.

A second large interest of Jefferson as reflected by its proportional representation in his collection, thirteen percent, was history. His historical collection emphasized the ancient history of Greece and Rome and the history of Great Britain and France. He had made a special effort, Jefferson said, to collect difficult-to-obtain works on the early settlement of America by foreign countries when he lived abroad.[119] This emphasis upon history is also seen in the libraries of such contemporaries of Jefferson as William Byrd (see table 5), John Adams (see table 4), Benjamin Franklin (see table 6), and even in the popular social libraries (see table 7), and in the college libraries (see table 8) of the time. These other libraries, in fact, had a larger percentage of their collection in history, although none except Harvard had as many historical titles as Jefferson. Few of them had as many historical works in original languages and as many primary source materials as Jefferson, who expressed a preference for "original authors to compilers . . . and . . . translations."[120]

This same preference for original works is seen in Jefferson's section on "Literature," which was twelve percent of his library (see table 4). This emphasis is comparable to that of other libraries of the time but the quality of Jefferson's literary collection is noteworthy. It was made up of many classical works in the original Greek and Latin as well as such outstanding titles in English as the works of Shakespeare and Milton. Jefferson objected to light fiction that did not teach a moral lesson and thought time spent reading novels might better be used in reading serious works.[121] Other contemporary libraries showed a much greater emphasis upon fiction, biography, and light literature than Jefferson's did. Jefferson's collection of literature is more comparable to the collections of the college libraries than those of the other contemporary libraries, indicating he first gained his interest in the classical world and in good literature while at college. The passages Jefferson selected to copy in his college literary commonplace notebook support this fact.[122] Jefferson, unlike many of his friends, continued his study of the classics all his life.[123]

That Jefferson had more cultivated artistic interests than the rest of his fellow Americans of the period is revealed by his library collection of works on the "Fine Arts." Although the seventy-nine titles so classified comprised only two percent of his library, that was a larger percentage than in the other contemporary libraries, which had one percent or less of their collections in art. Jefferson's collection on art reflected his special interests in architecture, sculpture, and performing music. His interest in the arts probably came from his early exposure to the Cavalier tastes of the royal governor's court in Williamsburg while he was attending college,[124] his desire to emulate Roman villa life at Monticello,[125] and the influence of his long residence in France.

Jefferson's library indicates an interest in science as a major emphasis, with 710 titles making up fourteen percent of the library (see table 4). Only the Harvard Library has as many titles (see table 8) and only Franklin's library has a greater percentage (see table 6). Jefferson's lifelong interest in promoting scientific knowledge, documented by his many writings and scientific pursuits,[126] came from his early experience with the American frontier and the American Indians, his belief in the importance of America's western lands, his love of nature, his interest in improving agriculture, and his Enlightenment conviction of the importance of scientific knowledge and the power of human reason as man's best hope for progress. Such beliefs were not original with Jefferson and he was not the only American to hold them, but both his writings and his library holdings prove that he was the outstanding American spokesman for scientific progress and Enlightenment liberalism of his time.

Jefferson's library holdings of "Theology" and "Philosophy" are less than the other libraries studied. They are much less than the college libraries, which fact is an indication of the church relationship of the first American colleges. Some scholars have maintained there was a larger interest in theology in Puritan New England and more liberal interests in general culture in Cavalier Virginia. Other scholars have argued that, while geographical and social differences did affect the culture of both states, Puritan New England had broader cultural interests and Cavalier Virginia had more interest in religion than has been generally recognized. A comparison of the libraries and the writings of John Adams and Thomas Jefferson (see table 4) does not indicate a significant difference of interest in religion. Thomas Jefferson indicated he had a lack of interest in disputing about theology and speculating about matters that no man could know,[127] while Adams was more fond of letting his mind rove into unexpected and original avenues of thought.[128] They were in agreement, however, about basic liberal and anti-Calvinistic religious beliefs.[129] The content of Jefferson's library on religion needs further study by scholars.

Jefferson's library does faithfully reflect the broad political, social, religious, and humanitarian concerns of this great

American, as well as his many scholarly interests. It reveals Jefferson as a highly intelligent and intellectual man for whom studying and reading were lifelong interests. The books of his library were, for Jefferson, both the essential tools of his work and the unfailing delight of his long life.

4

Religious Attitudes Seen in Jefferson's Library Collection

ALTHOUGH MUCH can be learned about the interests and convictions of Thomas Jefferson from the composition of his library and the relative size of its sections, to really understand his thought it is necessary to examine the works that influenced him title by title. Such a study would be rewarding, for he was a person who read widely, kept careful notes of his reading, and used his reading to develop his own thought. James Madison, Jefferson's close friend and associate, believed that Jefferson was "the most learned man that ever devoted so much time to public life."[1]

Jefferson, moreover, was a person of firm beliefs and strong convictions.[2] In the political field, a study of Jefferson's favorite authors on law and government helps explain some of his puzzling actions as president. Scholars have long wondered why he clung so strongly to his policy of neutrality and embargo during the Napoleonic Wars despite the obvious disadvantages to the United States.[3] Part of the reason is to be found in Jefferson's aversion to war based on his admiration for those authors of international law he had studied who taught that there was a moral code to be followed by nations as strictly as the moral code of individuals in which Jefferson believed so thoroughly.[4]

Studying important works in Jefferson's library, then, provides the historian with important clues to his character and beliefs. Since his library had 10,000 titles, such a study is beyond the scope of this work. A discussion of the important titles in one section of Jefferson's library and the insight they give into his thought, however, will be made. Since there has been so much controversy about Jefferson's religious beliefs[5] and so little objective study of his religion,[6] his library section on "Religion, Ethics, and Philosophy" is examined as a case study to show how Jefferson's reading in religion and ethics casts light upon his character and thinking.

Our study of Jefferson's reading interests based on the relative size of the classified sections of his library and on a comparison with the theological sections of other contemporary libraries seems to indicate that Jefferson had less interest in religion than did other leaders of his time. He protested, however, that he had long studied religious writers and was interested in the subject of religion.[7]

Several questions come to mind. Was Jefferson really a politically minded person largely uninterested in moral questions? Was he a scientifically inclined person with a materialistic point of view, uninterested in spiritual matters? As a Cavalier Virginian, was he opposed to Puritanism and Calvinism? What can a careful study of Thomas Jefferson's library tell us about his real religious attitudes? In order to answer these questions, the results of a study, title by title, of the relevant sections on religion in the main library which Jefferson sold to Congress, as described by E. Millicent Sowerby,[8] are presented in this chapter.

Jefferson's Classification of Religion, Ethics, Philosophy

In order to analyze the works on religion which Jefferson selected for his library, it is necessary to determine what should be included under the general heading religion. In the years since Jefferson collected and arranged his library, many of the terms included under religion, such as *ethics, morals, philosophy,* and *theology,* have changed their meaning. *Philosophy,* for example, was used by Jefferson and other thinkers of his time, particularly Francis Bacon, to include all branches of learning that involved the use of man's reason. Jefferson divided philosophy into two main divisions, "Moral Philosophy" and "Mathematical Philosophy." He further divided "Mathematical Philosophy" into the "Pure" mathematics of arithmetic and geometry and into the "Physico-mathematics" of applied scientific subjects (see table 1). Even under the classification of "Moral Philosophy," Jefferson distinguished between "Ethics," "Religion," "Law" (of many types), and "Oeconomical Jurisprudence" (which covered political and social science). Jefferson explained his classification to a friend, Judge Augustus Woodward:

> The latter ["Moral Philosophy"] includes ideology, ethics, and mental science generally; in my catalogue, considering ethics, as well as religion, as supplements to law in the government of man, I had placed them in that sequence.[9]

Thus spoke Jefferson the lawyer!

In a long letter to Peter Carr, Jefferson gave his thoughts on the subjects that should be offered in a complete program of education. As part of this program of education, he defined what subjects he considered part of the study of philosophy.

> In the Philosophical department, I should distinguish: (1) Ideology, (2) Ethics, (3) Law of Nature and Nations, (4) Government, (5) Political Economy.[10]

It is clear from these references that Jefferson was thinking of religion in a broad sense including ethics, and that, even when he was discussing philosophy in the modern sense of the word, he was thinking of it in a broad sense including logic and epistemology as well as value systems.

Koch, in her study of Thomas Jefferson's philosophy, followed Jefferson's division of philosophy into the subjects of ideology, ethics and personal morality, the Law of Nature and of Nations, and the study of society and government.[11] This arrangement has the advantage of growing naturally out of Jefferson's interests and thought but tends to obscure his religious beliefs and involves the study of political and social science.

Since the emphasis of this chapter is on Jefferson's religious thought, it is necessary to distinguish what materials in Jefferson's library may be properly considered to fall under the heading of religion today, in contrast to the wider use of the terms for ethics and philosophy by Jefferson. The Dewey Decimal Library Classification System lists under the general heading of "Religion" such subheadings as "Natural Religion," "Bible," "Doctrinal Theology," "Devotional," "Social Theology," "Church History," and "Other Religions," and lists "Ethics" or "Moral Philosophy" as a division under the "Philosophy" heading.[12] By using these subjects as a guide, the titles in Jefferson's library that would be classified under "Religion" today may be readily identified within the Baconian classification titles used by Jefferson for religious subjects. The book titles within the following subject classifications used by Jefferson will accordingly be discussed: "Chapter I, Antient History," "Chapter V, Ecclesiastical History," "Chapter XVI, Ethics—Moral Philosophy, and Ethics—Law of Nature and Nations," "Chapter XVII, Religion," and "Chapter XXII, Law—Ecclesiastical" (see table 3).

If these subject classifications seem somewhat remote from religion, it should be remembered that they show not only Jefferson's legal training and interests but also the religious interests of his day. Men of the Enlightenment were interested in finding a basis for morality, law, and society different from that of the medieval church. Grotius, Puffendorf, Wolf, Vattel, and other Enlightenment authors studied by Jefferson[13] led the way in separating the law of nature (*lex naturae*) from the law of God (*lex divina*). As Ernst Troeltsch comments:

> The investigations . . . of the Enlightenment . . . destroyed the idea of a history of the world based on Daniel, the Apocalypse, and St. Augustine, opened up vast realms of time, rejected the fall of man as the cardinal point in universal evolution, and created a new type of primitive man . . . [based on] natural law, religion, and morality; and all deviations from the norm were ascribed to evil or cunning, to tyranny or priestly hypocrisy, to stupidity or ignorance.[14]

Jefferson's arrangement of his books on religion in terms of church history, church law, and the innate moral laws found in nature and in human character and society is understandable in terms of his study of Enlightenment philosophy.

Church History

Jefferson's interest in the classical period reinforced his interest in the history of the early Christian church, since the Christian movement was part of Greco-Roman society and history. In all, Jefferson had 129 titles under "Antient History" and twenty-five under "Ecclesiastical History."

Under Ancient History he had three copies of the *Works of Josephus* (in Greek, Latin, and English), the Jewish historian for the period covering the life of Christ. He had several copies in Greek, Latin, and English of the works of the Greek historians, Thucydides, Xenophon, and Herodotus, as well as several English summary histories of Greece. He also had two copies of Plutarch's *Lives* in Greek and Latin.[15]

He had copies of the works of such Roman historians as Julius Caesar, Marcus Justinus, Lucius Florus, Dio Cassius, Appianus of Alexandria, and Cornelius Tacitus.[16] Jefferson thought very highly of Tacitus and wrote, "Tacitus I consider as the first writer in the world without a single exception. His book is a compound of history and morality of which we have no other example."[17]

For general works of ancient history Jefferson included Oliver Goldsmith's *Roman History*, Edward Gibbon's *The Decline and Fall of the Roman Empire*, and the works of the French historians Charles Le Beau, Chronicon Paschale, and Rene-Aubert de Vertot.[18] Jefferson also listed under "Antient History" a Greek-Latin and French translation of *The Lives and Opinions of Famous Philosophers* by Diogenes of Laertius, the most important of early collections of Greek philosophy. He also had an English version by Thomas Stanley[19] based on Diogenes' writings.

In the section of his library which he called "Ecclesiastical History," Jefferson had seven works of church history, including the works of such early church historians as Eusebius, Socrates Scholasticus, and Theodoretus. These works were in French or Latin. Jefferson also listed two accounts of church councils (those of Florence and Trent), five works on the lives of the Popes, some critical, two works on the lives of saints or bishops, and one history of the Crusades in French.[20] He frequently used his study of the early church to prove that more complicated theological doctrines such as the Trinity were "corruptions" of Jesus' simple teachings by later church leaders, such as Athanasius.[21]

One work on the Bible was listed as *A New History of the Holy Bible, from the Beginning of the World, to the Establishment of Christianity . . . The whole illustrated with proper Maps and Sculptures* by the Reverend Thomas Stackhouse, A.M. Late Vicar of Neenham. This work may have had some sentimental value for Jefferson as it was bequeathed to him by his friend and mentor, George Wythe, with whom he studied law.[22]

To these early works on church history, Jefferson added such works on the later history of the church as Bede's *History of the Church of England*, Gilbert Brunet's *History of the Reformation of the Church of England*, and *The Historie of the Reformation of the Church of Scotland* by John Knox.[23] A favorite historical work which Jefferson frequently recommended was a six-volume history by Johann Lorenz von Mosheim, Chancellor of the University of Göttingen. Although it was titled, *An Ecclesiastical History, Antient and Modern*, it clearly was valued as being broader than that since it covered such things as the voyages of Columbus and Vasquez de Gama and the invention of printing.[24] Other reference works which Jefferson included were a collection on the lives of English bishops, a *Description of the Religious and Military Orders*, and a *History and Fate of Sacrilege*, "now published for the Terror of Evil Doers."[25]

Ethics—Moral Philosophy

Jefferson divided his collection of works on ethics into two sections. The first section, which he called "Moral Philosophy," numbered 138 titles and was one of the most important parts of his library, containing many works that were important in shaping his thought and which he often quoted to his friends. Here are to be found most of the well-known writers of the Enlightenment, both English and French. Many of them were close friends of Jefferson. For example, the second entry is *Ideologie* by Destutt de Tracy, of whom Jefferson wrote to his friend John Adams, "Destutt-Tracy, is in my judgment, the ablest writer living on intellectual subjects, or the operations of the understanding."[26]

Jefferson also had works on the process of thought by Bacon, Locke, Cabanis, Condorcet, and Dugald Stewart, another personal friend. All of these works reflect Jefferson's interest in exploring the material means by which men think. They influenced him strongly towards a materialistic understanding of the nature of man.[27] Jefferson did have, however, a work taking an opposing position, *The Nature of the Human Soul* by Andrew Baxter, a Scotch philosopher, among these titles.[28]

Jefferson was greatly influenced by the deist writers of his time and had many of their works in his collection. The American deists were represented by the writings of Elihu Palmer, founder of deist societies in New York and other cities, Joshua Peel, and Ethan Allen, known for his revolutionary activities in Vermont.[29] The English deists were even more important in shaping Jefferson's thought, and in his library are found the works of Bolingbroke, Lord Kames, Matthew Tindal, Thomas Chubb, William Dudgeon, Peter Arnet, Charles Blount, Lord Shaftesbury, Thomas Hobbes, Bernard Mandeville, and David Hume.[30]

Jefferson copied in his notes on his reading long passages from Lord Shaftesbury's writings on the foolishness of governments' trying to enforce uniformity of opinion and customs, especially in matters of religion.[31] He often echoed these ideas in his own writings.[32]

John Locke's works also greatly influenced Jefferson. He copied long passages from Locke's *Letter Concerning Toleration* in his commonplace notebook,[33] and used many of Locke's ideas and phrases in his own writings on the need for religious freedom.[34] Jefferson, however, wanted to "go on" from Locke's idea of tolerating only certain less objectionable religions to the radical step of complete freedom for all religious ideas and separation of church and state.[35] Jefferson likewise was influenced in writing the Declaration of Independence by his readings in Locke's writings on the rights of men to "life, liberty, and property" and their being "by nature all free, equal, and independent."[36]

Another important teaching of the English deists which Jefferson early adopted as a most important article of his own religious belief was that a religion based on reason and science was superior to one based on blind faith and supernatural revelation.[37] He thus followed the rational explanation of the Bible and its miracles which he had read in the works of Blount and Thomas Hobbes,[38] although he disagreed with Hobbes that primitive man formed a "social compact" to create society from a lawless state. Jefferson thought all men, including savages, respected moral right.[39]

It was the eighteenth-century deist philosopher, Henry Saint-John, Viscount Bolingbroke, who most influenced Jefferson towards a rationalistic and skeptical view of religion. He told Adams that he had read Bolingbroke "for the first time fifty years ago, and not less than five times since."[40] He copied long passages from Bolingbroke in his commonplace book on the superiority of a religion based on reason to one based on miracles.[41] Bolingbroke's attacks on dogmatic religion[42] are also reflected in Jefferson's arguments on the subject.[43]

Jefferson also gained from his study of the deists his interest in comparative religions and cultures. He wrote to Adams concerning the religious truths followed by the five-sixths of the world that had a different revelation from the Christian one,[44] an idea that he found in his reading of Matthew Tindal.[45] From his reading in the deist writings Jefferson was also influenced towards a strong Unitarian view of Christianity which he frequently expressed to friends when he was writing about religion.[46]

The French atheists are also represented in Jefferson's library, which fact was one of the grounds for accusing Jefferson of being an atheist and for opposing the purchase of his library by Congress.[47] Besides the work of the famous Voltaire, which Jefferson seems to have used more for factual information than inspiration,[48] he had factual works by Diderot, writer for the French Encyclopédie.[49]

Jefferson admired the scientific spirit of the Encyclopedists and wrote articles on wildlife in America for them.[50] Other French atheists and deists whose works are found in Jefferson's library are D'Holbach, Boulanger, Pierre Bayle, Volney, and Montaigne, as well as that Italian freethinker, Lucilio Vanini.[51] Many of these writers were persecuted for their writings by the entrenched European churches and monarchies. Jefferson commented on their philosophy to his friend John Adams:

> I always supposed . . . Grimm to be of the school of Diderot, D'Alembert, D'Holbach . . . of atheism. . . . It was a numerous school in the Catholic countries, while the infidelity of the Protestant took generally the form of Theism.[52]

That Jefferson was no atheist but a firm believer in God is amply proven by his writings to friends,[53] and by his many references to "God," "the Deity," "Creator," "Father," and "Holy Author of our religion" in his public addresses and writings.[54] The clearest reflection of his deist readings is found in the following passage written to Adams near the end of his life:

> I hold . . . that when we take a view of the universe, . . . the movements of the heavenly bodies, so exactly held in their courses by the balance of centrifugal and centripetal forces; the structure of our earth itself, with its distribution of lands, waters, and atmosphere; animal and vegetable bodies, examined in all their minutest particles, . . . it is impossible, I say, for the human mind not to believe, that there is in all this, design, cause and effect, up to an ultimate cause, a Fabricator of all things from matter and motion.[55]

Jefferson was influenced in forming this conviction of God as Originator of life and Creator of the universe by his readings in Shaftesbury and Bolingbroke, for he quoted passages from their writings in his commonplace books to this effect.[56] He also was guided by Claude Adrien Helvetius' work *De l'homme* in his tolerant understanding of the difference between deists and atheists, as indicated by a passage from Helvetius that he copied in his commonplace book.[57]

Reflecting his keen interest in the classical writers which he studied in college and continued to read with pleasure all his life,[58] Jefferson had an extensive collection of the works of his favorite Greek and Roman moral philosophers, including the

following: Hierocles of Alexandria, a Neoplatonist writer; four
works by Epictetus and two by Theophrastus; two by Marcus
Aurelius Antonius, one by Aeschines Socraticus, the Athenian
philosopher; *The Memoirs of Socrates*, including his defense
and death, by Xenophon; and Aristotles' *Ethica*.[59] In this same
section of his library were copies of Plutarch's works on *Ethics*
and *Morals*, Cato's *Moral Admonitions*, and seven copies of
various works of Cicero, whom Jefferson greatly admired both
as a thinker and as a person, as well as three works of Seneca.[60]
Among the lesser known Greek and Roman philosophers, Jefferson had works by Boethius, Felix Minucius, Alexander of
Aphrodisius, Philostratus, and Maximus Tyrius.[61]

The influence of these classical writers upon Jefferson can
scarcely be overemphasized. Their somber yet brave understanding of death, immortality, and fate made an early and
lasting influence upon Jefferson's thought.[62] His study of the
Stoic philosophers gave Jefferson a lifelong courage and per-
sistance in courses he believed right despite misunderstanding
and opposition. The Stoic ideal of "the noble Roman" using
his talents and resources in the service of his country and fellow
man also deeply influenced Jefferson.[63] The philosophy of
Epicurus provided direction for Jefferson in the pursuit of
happiness, which he saw as the purpose of life,[64] but he was
influenced by the Enlightenment Epicurean French author and
priest Pierre Gassendi, Jefferson wrote, to see happiness as a
self-disciplined enjoyment of the finer and more worthwhile
activities of study and service.[65] Jefferson's tastes in art and
architecture were shaped by his classical readings so much that
he consciously recreated in his home at Monticello the setting and
life of a noble Roman aristocrat, Karl Lehmann demonstrates.[66]
Jefferson greatly admired the moral codes of the Greeks and
Romans, even more than Old Testament laws, although he
looked upon Jesus as the "greatest moralist who ever lived."[67]
He wrote:

> Let a just view be taken of the moral principles . . . of
> ancient philosophy; particularly Pythagoras, Socrates,
> Epicurus, Cicero, Epictetus, Seneca, Antonius. . . . Their
> precepts related chiefly to ourselves, and the government
> of those passions which, unrestrained, would disturb our

tranquility of mind. In this branch of philosophy they were really great. . . . In developing our duties to others, they were short and defective.[68]

In this same section of his library Jefferson had three copies of the works of Plato.[69] Lest the unwary investigator conclude their inclusion indicates a fondness for Plato, Jefferson wrote on numerous occasions of his distaste for Plato's abstract speculations. A fair sample is his letter to William Short in which he comments sarcastically on "the whimsies of Plato's own foggy brain. . . . No writer antient [sic] or modern has bewildered the world with more *ignes fatui* than this renowned philosopher in Ethics, in Politics and Physics."[70]

Jefferson had several general works on the history of philosophy and on the philosophy of nature in his library. Two that he especially valued were Abbé Charles Batteux's work detailing the teachings of early philosophers, and William Enfield's *History of Philosophy* which reduced to one English volume Brucker's earlier multivolume work in Latin.[71] Jefferson praised Enfield for giving a "detailed account of the opinions and principles of the different sects [as] these relate to the gods, their natures, grades, places and powers." He used it as the basis of his discussion on comparative religions with Adams.[72]

One unfortunate influence which Jefferson absorbed from his reading of Enfield's version of moral philosophy and from other Enlightenment writers, which he quoted to Adams in this letter, was a belief that the moral philosophy of the Jews was degraded and excessively legalistic. Jefferson had copied Bolingbroke's *Philosophical Works* which also argued that the teachings of Moses revealed a "degraded," "familiar," "unjust and cruel" idea of God and taught an unworthy, unbelievable, and uncertain law to a "little known and contemned people . . . shut up in a little corner of the world."[73]

Further reflecting his interest in comparative religion, Jefferson had Dupuis' work *Origin of the Cults* in his library collection. The later moral philosophers are represented by the works of Spinoza, Kant, and Swedenberg.[74] He also had several books and tracts on "manners and morals," four general works on ethics, three on theology, and a stray *Commentary on the Gospel of Luke*.[75]

[125]

A last, and most interesting, section of Jefferson's library on "Moral Philosophy" was a collection of nineteen titles on the evils of slavery and the slave trade, the problems of the Negroes in various parts of the world, and the question of their intellectual and artistic capabilities.[76] Some of these works were in French by French idealists. To one of them, Jefferson wrote concerning his own studies and conclusions:

> You know that nobody wishes more ardently to see an abolition not only of the trade but of the condition of slavery: and certainly nobody will be more willing to encounter every sacrifice for that object.[77]

These works show Jefferson's concern with the evils of slavery and influenced him to propose various measures to end it in the United States.[78] They also provided ideas and material for his numerous and eloquent writings against slavery.[79] For example, in the margin of his copy of Lord Kames's *Essays on the Principles of Morality and Natural Religion* which condemned the killing of captives taken in war, Jefferson condemned also making slaves of them.[80]

Ethics—Law of Nature and Nations

The second section of Jefferson's library on ethics, "Law of Nature and Nations," grew naturally out of his study of the basis of law in human society and out of his conviction that there was one moral law written into the world of nature and into the character of men. The moral law governed men's actions both as individuals and as nations and was fundamental to the study of law. It was also the basis of all ethics. These beliefs were the rationale for the close connection of religion, ethics, and law in his library and curriculum of studies, Jefferson stated.[81]

In this section on "Law of Nature and Nations," comprising sixty-eight titles, are to be found some of Jefferson's favorite authors' works on the origin and nature of law and society, such as Hugo Grotius, *Le Droit de la Guerre et de la Paix*, Samuel von Puffendorf, *The Law of Nature and Nations*, Christian Wolf, *Institutions du Droit de la Nature et des Gens* (in Latin and French), and Emeric de Vattel, *Droit des Gens* and *Questions de Droit Naturel.*[82] When President George Washington asked his cabinet for advice on the question of whether the treaty of the United States with France was still binding after the change of government caused by the French Revolution, Jefferson quoted long passages from these works on the moral obligations of nations, indicating their influence upon his thought.[83]

In his collection on the "Law of Nature," Jefferson included works by Jean Burlamaqui, William Dodd, Fortunatio Felice, and Richard Cumberland, all elaborating the Enlightenment idea of the moral law which occurs in nature and in the hearts of men.[84] Jefferson was greatly influenced by his studies of the natural moral law, and he adopted the philosophy expounded by these authors of the basically moral nature of law. His studies in law, combined with his studies of the moral basis of human society and government, gave Jefferson's political convictions a religious and moral basis which is often overlooked by modern historians. Jefferson argued throughout his life that men were intended to live together in society, that social life was impossible without just government, and that social justice was possible only because man was endowed with a sense of right and wrong by his Creator.[85] Jefferson's readings in moral law also led him to state often that moral beliefs and ethical behavior were the most important part of religion, much more important than the dogma and theology that divided religious people into warring factions.[86]

The influence of Jefferson's library studies in "Ethics" is well illustrated by an essay on his moral ideas which Jefferson wrote to a friend, Thomas Law. The account was written in response to Law's new book, *Second Thoughts on Instinctive Impulses,* which the author had sent to Jefferson,[87] who was constantly receiving works from aspiring authors.

In this case Jefferson mentioned taking the book to his summer home for leisurely reading.[88] In his retirement, he enjoyed the extra leisure his visits to his place at Poplar Forest afforded for reading, his family remembered.[89] He even duplicated some of the favorite works of his library in more portable editions, "petit format," in order to have them there to study.[90]

This essay shows Jefferson's use of authorities, and the ease with which he drew upon his wide reading to review the varied theories of morality. Some he mentioned and rejected, such as Wollaston's theory that truth was the foundation of man's morality.[91] Lord Kames's idea of impulsive feeling or compassion as the basis of morality he accepted but, since it was a minor point, he quoted it from memory, although he stated that it was "fifty years since I read his book."[92] The theory he most agreed with, that of Helvetius that men instinctively love the good and wish to alleviate evil, he quoted exactly, and it is clear that he had the book open before him as he wrote.[93] Even with the writings of Helvetius, one can see Jefferson changing, adapting, and further developing the thought as he integrated the ideas from many writers together and modified them all in the light of his own wide experience with men and society. One can easily picture Jefferson at work at his writing desk in his library with many opened books scattered around him just as his slave, Isaac Jefferson, remembered him.[94]

In the section of his library on the moral law of nations, Jefferson also had twenty-two titles dealing with various treaties among nations and eight works concerning the quarrels of nations, as well as two works of maritime law dealing with the rights of nations at sea. These titles reflected Jefferson's professional interest in law and statesmanship. He had, in addition, nine works describing the rights, duties and rules of conduct for ambassadors representing their nation to another one, which reflected his professional needs when he was the American representative to France.[95]

Religion

This section has 271 titles, more than any of the other sections in Jefferson's library on religious subjects. The largest and most important collection within this classification was Jefferson's collection of Bibles. For a man with a reputation for being irreligious he had an amazing number! He had two copies in Greek of the Septuagint, that early Greek translation of the Hebrew Old Testament; he had ten copies of the whole Bible in the Latin Vulgate version; and ten copies of various Greek New Testaments, some with parallel columns of Latin, and another one with Greek, Latin and French. For lighter reading Jefferson had one copy of the Bible in French and six in English.[96] One of these was the first translation of the Septuagint into English by his friend Charles Thomson, to whom Jefferson wrote:

> I thank you, my dear and antient [sic] friend, for the two volumes of your translation which you have been so kind to send me. I propose . . . to give to the Septuagint an attentive perusal, and shall feel the aid you have now given me.[97]

Thomson's work and the interest of friends with whom he corresponded did encourage Jefferson to undertake extensive study of the Bible, especially during his later years, as is indicated not only by this library collection of Bibles but by the fact that he also had three English New Testaments, five Greek New Testaments, four in Greek and Latin, and one in Greek and English.[98]

Indicating a special interest were copies of the single books of Job, Isaiah, and Psalms.[99] The book of Psalms was always a favorite of Jefferson's, partly because of his long familiarity with the Episcopal book of worship and his fondness for private devotions.[100] He frequently quoted psalms to his family and friends as models for one's life, especially the ones that described a good person.[101] To John Adams, Jefferson quoted Psalms 18 and 148 as the loftiest expressions of religion he knew, and displayed a remarkable knowledge of various translations of them, based on his extensive library collection.[102]

Among his Bible collection, Jefferson had four copies of the complete Apocrypha and four copies of various single Apocryphal books.[103] That Jefferson was influenced to hold some skepticism of Biblical authority from his readings in the Apocrypha is indicated in a letter to his nephew Peter Carr:

> I forgot to observe when speaking of the New Testament that you should read all the histories of Christ, . . . those whom a council of ecclesiastics have decided for us to be Pseudo-evangelists, as well as those they named Evangelists. . . . Most of these are lost. There are some however still extant, collected by Fabricius which I will endeavor to get and send you.[104]

Fabricius' work was in Jefferson's library.[105]

Among his reference works for studying the Bible, Jefferson listed five commentaries on the Bible, such as John Brown's *Dictionary of the Holy Bible . . . forming a Sacred Commentary; a body of Scripture History, Chronology, And Divinity; and serving in a great measure as a Concordance to the Bible.*[106] In addition were four different concordances to the Bible, including the one by Alexander Cruden which is still used today.[107] Other works for reference were two *Histories of the Holy Land* and one work entitled *The History of our Blessed Lord and Saviour Jesus Christ: with the Lives of the Holy Apostles, and their successors for three hundred years after the Crucifixion.*[108] In a letter to the publisher, Jefferson expressed his opinion of this work:

> It comprehends exactly the most interesting period of Christian history. . . . I presume it . . . gives the primitive and earlier opinions entertained, being persuaded that nothing would place Christianity on so firm a base as the reducing it simply to its first and original principles.[109]

Jefferson had two other works of interpretation of Jesus and three on the *Resurrection of Jesus.*

Another Biblical reference work, and one that exerted considerable influence upon Jefferson, was Joseph Priestley's *Harmony of the Evangelists,* which Jefferson went to some trouble to procure, finally obtaining a personal copy from Priestley himself.[110] According to Sowerby, the work was in two volumes, the first containing Priestley's *Observations on the Harmony of the Evangelists* in English and the second the *Harmony* itself in Greek and English compared.[111]

Priestley's volumes stimulated Jefferson in his work on a similar project of making "a digest of his [Jesus'] moral doctrines, extracted in his own words from the Evangelists," Jefferson wrote to Priestley.[112] Jefferson had long desired such an extract of Jesus' life and moral teachings. He related:

> I had sent to Philadelphia to get two testaments (Greek) of the same edition, and two English, with a design to cut out the morsels of morality, and paste them on the leaves

of a book, in the manner you describe as having been pursued in forming your Harmony.[113]

Many years later these two mutilated New Testaments turned up in a collection of books purchased from Jefferson's library by an enthusiast, and Cyrus Adler, librarian for the Smithsonian Institution, succeeded in locating and publishing "the morsels of morality" which Jefferson had compiled as his famous "Bible."[114]

Another favorite study project of Jefferson "was the task of comparing the moral doctrines of Jesus with those of the ancient Philosophers," which he urged Priestley to do.[115] Priestley followed Jefferson's suggestion and completed such a comparison of Christianity with earlier religions before his death, much to Jefferson's satisfaction.[116] Jefferson had been stimulated in his interest in this subject by an earlier study by Priestley comparing the life and teachings of Jesus and Socrates, he wrote to Benjamin Rush. Jefferson never had the time to do the research necessary for as full a study as he envisioned, but he did send to Rush and other friends an essay outlining his ideas comparing the morals of Jesus with those of Socrates, Seneca, and other classical moralists, as well as those of the Jews.[117]

The subject of comparative religion, which Jefferson, like other Enlightenment thinkers, found of great interest, is further represented in this section of his library by three titles on the early Greek and Roman religions, another work on comparative religions, and one copy of the Koran.[118] He also had four more short works by Priestley on religion which were bound together with some other religious essays under the general title of *Theological Pamphlets*.[119]

Jefferson also had seven works interpreting the Bible (besides his large collection of sermons) on prophecy, the Apocalypse, the millenium, and the books of Daniel and Revelation.[120] One interesting work was a collection of children's Bible stories in Latin, perhaps used for catechism instruction, first printed in Switzerland in the sixteenth century.[121] He had ten works on theology ranging from Catholic, Protestant, and Eastern Church apologetics to William Penn's famous work *No Cross, No Crown* in French.[122] Here too were works explaining various sects, such as the Moravian, Quaker, Anabaptist and

United Brethren, as well as several about the Unitarians,[123] towards which Jefferson leaned because of his agreement with Priestley, who was prominent in the Unitarian religious movement in England and started the Unitarian Society in Philadelphia.[124]

Most of Priestley's scientific and religious writings are found in Jefferson's library. Particularly influential on Jefferson's thought were Priestley's *An History of the Corruptions of Christianity* and *An History of early opinions concerning Jesus Christ, compiled from Original Writers; proving that the Christian Church was at first Unitarian.*[125] Commenting on *The Corruptions of Christianity*, Jefferson wrote to a friend, "The work of Dr. Priestley which I sent you has always been a favorite of mine." Jefferson believed, he added, that Priestley's work proved:

> The doctrines of Jesus as delivered by himself . . . contain the outlines of the sublimest system of morality that has ever been taught but . . . corruptions of it . . . have been invented by priestcraft and established by kingcraft constituting a conspiracy of church and state against the civile and religious liberties of mankind.[126]

After John Adams accused Jefferson of not reading much on religious subjects, including the theology of Priestley, Jefferson replied that the works of Priestley just discussed and the works of Conyers Middleton, "especially his letters from Rome and to Waterland [were] *the basis of my own faith*" (italics mine).[127] Jefferson had Middleton's complete *Miscellaneous Works* in his library.[128] Middleton was a liberal professor and librarian of Cambridge University. He argued in his works that the teachings of the Catholic Church contained many ideas from Roman paganism, that there were many contradictions in the New Testament which could not be reconciled, and that the story of the fall of man was a fable.[129] Jefferson's writings reflect many of these criticisms,[130] and he always believed that the fall of mankind was into ignorance which could be overcome by the spread of education.[131]

Jefferson was quite correct in stating that he was deeply influenced by the researches of Priestley whom he read "over and over again" for his "learning, so much superior to my own."[132]

[132]

Priestley's studies in the writings of the early church fathers indicating that Trinitarian theology and the exalted, spiritual belief about the figure of Jesus Christ were later "corruptions" of the earlier, simpler teachings of Jesus convinced Jefferson and he repeated the argument in many of his own writings.[133] Jefferson likewise agreed with Priestley's scientific approach to man and his world and adopted his argument that man was composed of matter, not spirit, as Plato and later theologians argued.[134] Jefferson also stressed the Unitarian emphasis upon Jesus as a great moralist and teacher,[135] rather than a spiritual God.[136] The literary evidence indicates that Jefferson was more influenced in his religious convictions by Priestley's writings than by any other author.

Another group of titles in Jefferson's library classified under "Religion" was numerous prayer books, "Books of Hours," and works of meditation for Anglicans, Catholics, and Dissenters.[137] Jefferson had several *Catechisms*, several titles on the sacrament of the Lord's supper, one on *The Festivals and Fasts of the Church of England*, one on *The Thirty-Nine Articles of the Church of England*, and one on Christian education.[138] These works reflect Jefferson's early Anglican training and long attendance at the services of the Church of England from which he developed a lifelong custom of personal devotions.[139]

The most important of the early Church Fathers' original works, mostly in Latin, made up another large section of Jefferson's religious library. There were the works of Origen, Ignatius, Clement of Alexandria, and Justin Martyr. He had the *Confessions of St. Augustine* and Thomas à Kempis's *Imitations of Christ*. Also in his collection were works by St. Gregory, Tertullianus, Philo, the Jewish philosopher who interpreted Greek thought, and Theodoretus and Eusebius, the historians. In all there were twenty such titles.[140] This collection reflects Jefferson's interest in studying for himself the development of the early Christian church and of Christian doctrines. The "corruptions" of the early "primitive" faith of Jesus by later "priestcraft," as Jefferson termed it, was an important article of Jefferson's Enlightenment beliefs. The influence of these works is proven by his frequently citing ideas from the church fathers, occasionally quoting from them in Greek and Latin.[141]

Jefferson also had several works by Calvin, including an early

French copy of his *Institutions of Religion* and an early Latin and Greek edition of his *Rudiments of the Faith* and his *Catechism*, plus two works on the history of Calvinism.[142] The presence of these works in his library does not mean that Jefferson was influenced by them, except in a negative sense, for Jefferson made no secret of his vehement opposition to the doctrines of Calvin.[143] In a letter to John Adams, he called Calvin "an Atheist" and "his religion . . . Daemonism."[144] This remark shows the influence of Helvetius' book *De l'homme* upon Jefferson, for he had copied in his commonplace book Helvetius' comment to the effect that, judging by the cruel theology many people attributed to God, it was "the devil that the people adore under the name of God."[145] The presence of Calvin's works in Jefferson's library simply shows that he believed in studying well the works of his opponents in order to be able to refute them.

Next in his library section on "Religion," Jefferson had fifty-two theological works. These ranged from short pamphlets to multivolumed theological systems, and were written by theologians of every religious persuasion from German Lutherans, Scottish Presbyterians, English Anglicans, Eastern Churchmen, Dutch Protestants, and French abbés to English Puritans, Cambridge dons, and the Archibishop of Canterbury John Tillotson.[146] There were works supporting and attacking various religious faiths. On Roman Catholicism, Jefferson had a book of Catholic instruction for Protestants by a theological professor of Paris and another work entitled *The Romish Horseleech: or, An Impartial Account of . . . Popery. . . .*[147] There were accounts attacking and defending the beliefs of the Moravians, Anabaptists, United Brethren, and the Quakers.[148] The theological ideas discussed ran the gamut from salvation, the creeds, Platonism, God's pardon, the meaning of Calvary, prophecy, providence, the sanctity of God, justification, and the millenium.[149]

A notable group of ten titles concerned the subject of the soul and the body, death, mourning, the resurrection, eternity and suicide.[150] Jefferson's literary notebook contains many quotations on death, immortality, and fate from classical and literary authors, confirming his interest in this topic.[151]

Jefferson also had a further collection of works on English

deism in this section of his library. One was a three-volume work written to answer deistic ideas by William Warburton, Bishop of Gloucester, which was followed by two works by Arthur Sykes answering the bishop.[152] Jefferson also had two radical French works by Chaix de Sourcesol. Sowerby explains:

> Chaix de Sourcesol, one of the "fanatics of Avignon," a married priest, wrote against the Roman Church, the cult of relics and images, the invocation of the Saints, eternal punishment, ecclesiastical celibacy and other doctrines. He sent his books to Jefferson . . . and corresponded with him.[153]

Jefferson also included the essays of John Hildrop which were directed partly against the deists, two works defending the Bible and Christianity against Edward Gibbon's arguments in *The History of the Decline and Fall of the Roman Empire*, one book arguing that the Bible needed no defense, and two other titles answering the "false reasoning" of Thomas Paine's *Age of Reason*.[154] At the end of this library section Jefferson had filed six more copies of the Bible and the New Testament.[155]

Surprisingly enough, Jefferson had only three short works on the subject of religious toleration, religious liberty, and the separation of church and state.[156] He plainly had more interest in the subject of religious freedom than these few titles would indicate, since he studied and wrote extensively on the subject.[157] Instead of collecting and using much of what was being written in his time in the nature of opinions and arguments on religious freedom, Jefferson went to more basic sources among his authors on early church history, moral philosophy, political theory, and law.[158] John Locke's *Toleration* and Milton's writings on religion were particularly important in influencing his thought, Jefferson's notes on his reading on religion reveal.[159]

Thirteen works on the Christian's duty, morals, manners, and instructions for a gentleman and a lady make up a curious section of Jefferson's library of religious works.[160] It seems strange to the modern reader to note that one work on *Manners* by the French author Francois Vincent Toussaint was condemned to be burned.[161] It would seem the moral customs of the establishment have always been a controversial subject. Jefferson always taught his children that courtesy was based on Christian kindness and morality.[162]

Although, as we have seen, it has been argued that the Virginian gentlemen and freethinkers, such as Jefferson, did not have as many theological works and sermons in their libraries as the New England Puritans, it turns out that Jefferson had more sermons in the religious section of his library than any other type of work. There were sixty titles in all, ranging from short tracts to titles comprising several thick volumes, such as *The Works of the Rev. John Witherspoon, D.D., L.L.D., late President of the College, at Princeton, New Jersey* in three volumes and John Tillotson's *Sermons* in three volumes. Tillotson was Archibishop of Canterbury. Samuel Clarke, rector of St. James, Westminster, was represented by his *Sermons* in ten volumes on "faith in God, the unity of God, the eternity of God." Other collections of sermons ran to two and four volumes. The *Sermons* of Father Bourdaloue of the Company of Jesus and of Jean Baptiste Massillon of the French Academy extended to seventeen and fifteen volumes, respectively, in French. Among the shorter works, Jefferson had bound together in one volume two sermons preached in Christ Church, Philadelphia, and one by Ezra Stiles, President of Yale College, whom Jefferson liked, with a unitarian tract by Priestley and some other dissenter tracts.[163]

The authors whose sermons Jefferson collected were mostly Anglican clergymen but there were also Presbyterian, Congregational, Catholic, Unitarian, Dutch Protestant, Episcopalian, and Quaker clergy.[164] The sermons were sometimes preached for such special occasions as Thanksgiving Day, a fast day for peace, the Fourth of July, New Year's Day, or in the presence of the President and the Congress or a state legislature, and for funerals of important men.[165]

The sermons were preached on a wide variety of topics. Some were on theological subjects, such as God, love and charity, virtue, good and evil, prophecy, immortality, the resurrection of Lazarus, the Trinity, and the second coming of Christ.[166] Some sermons were on daily living, concerning themselves with social virtues and morality.[167] Other sermons were concerned with the religious issues of the times, such as the superiority of Mosaic institutions, the doctrines of different denominations, natural religion, the danger of revival services, and the falsity of the doctrine of universal salvation.[168] Other sermons were inspired by current events, such as those dealing with how to prevent war, how to maintain American unity and happiness, the nature of American patriotism, the issue of slavery, and one protesting the British attack on the American frigate, "Chesapeake."[169]

Jefferson acquired his sermons in a variety of ways. Some were learned works that he ordered from London or brought home from Paris. Some were gifts from the author or from a reader. Some were sent to convert him from his infidel ways, as was the case of the one accompanied by the following anonymous letter:

> Respected Friend,
> I entreat you to prepare to meet your God. For it will be but a short time before you must stand before his bar to answer for all the deeds done here below. And O may God grant that . . . you may become a sincere penitent before you leave the world. Farewell.[170]

Rev. David Austin sent two sermons to President Jefferson in Washington, "price fifty cents each," along with a request to be appointed "Librarian." Jefferson bought and dutifully filed his small purchase but refused the appointment with some sharpness since he had been repeatedly annoyed by the persistent minister.[171]

In this collection of sermons Jefferson also had a variety of religious pamphlets which he had filed with the sermons, binding them together in convenient volumes as he acquired them, without regard to any particular topic. Some were tracts but others were reports to various religious organizations, the minutes of their meetings, or sermons preached before them. There were reports of missionary societies organized to take the gospel to India, Africa, Asia, or to the American Indians. Other meetings reported were those of the Presbyterian church, several Baptist associations, yearly Friends' meetings, Unitarian meetings in Philadelphia, and the Female Charitable Society.[172]

In analyzing Jefferson's library collection in the section classified "Religion," one is impressed with the extent and variety of his collection. The collection of sermons and theological works is larger than one would expect, considering Jefferson's often expressed disinterest in religious disputations, but has a wide impartiality in line with his spirit of toleration. His collection of Bibles, reference works for studying the Bible, titles on church history, and works of devotion are surprisingly extensive and detailed.

Ecclesiastical Law

The last section of Jefferson's library that shows his interest in religious affairs is the section on ecclesiastical law which Jefferson classified as a subdivision of his law library. In all there were nineteen works classified "Law—Ecclesiastical." The majority of them, ten in number, dealt with the laws of the Anglican church under such titles as *Ecclesiastical Law, The Practice of Ecclesiastical Courts,* and *The Statutes, Constitutions, Canons, Rubricks and Articles of the Church of England.*[173] Jefferson had four titles that summarized the law for clergymen, giving "the duties and rights of the clergy" and advising on *The Law of Tythes.*[174] There were two works concerning the effect of the "municipall" or secular laws upon "spiritual power and jurisdiction."[175]

In addition to these law books on ecclesiastical law in general, Jefferson had four books concerning the laws governing last wills and testaments, one discussing "spousals or matrimonial contracts," and one on divorce with the provocative title of *The Case of Impotency Debated, in the late famous Tryal at Paris between the Marquis de Gesvres and his lady, Mademoiselle de Mascranny.*[176] The outcome of this early case of women's rights was not indicated.

These books on ecclesiastical law do more than indicate Jefferson's interest in the Church of England to which he belonged and the thoroughness of his study of all branches of law. They indicate the extent of the mixture of civil and ecclesiastical law in England during the eighteenth century and how strong was the effect of established religion upon the laws that governed the people of England and of the English colonies in America. Jefferson studied church law concerning marriage, divorce, and last wills and testaments because it was then the law of the land. The church laws on tithing were enforced by the civil police. Similarly, the laws of the different colonies and later American states concerning worship and conduct on the Sabbath had the force of law.[177] Jefferson was one of the first and most influential American leaders to work for the separation of civil and religious law.[178] As early as 1776 Jefferson was writing, "A church is a voluntary society of men," with the power to regulate its own affairs and beliefs but not those of all the people or society.[179] The legal power of the Anglican church revealed by Jefferson's books on ecclesiastical law help the modern reader understand their influence upon his thought and why Jefferson was so adamant about the separation of church and state in America.

Further evidence of Jefferson's study of the issue of the separation of civil and religious law is offered by six works on the problem that Jefferson had listed in the section of his library classified "Common Law." One of the arguments used in favor of the church establishment and of enforcing religion and morality by the civil law was that the laws of the Bible and morality were part of the English common law and hence part of the law of the land. Jefferson refuted this argument, after much study of his legal authorities, in a long essay which he sent to several friends on separate occasions.[180] The works in his library summarizing common law indicate his thorough study of the law, and two titles comparing "civil, canon and common law" bear directly on his concern with the problem.[181]

Summary and Conclusions

When Jefferson's library is carefully searched for titles with religious content and when the somewhat archaic subject classifications used by Jefferson are properly understood, it is seen that Jefferson had a greater interest in religious subjects and a larger religious collection than superficial comparisons of title numbers with other libraries might indicate. Classified under "Antient History" and "Ecclesiastical History" Jefferson had an extensive collection, mostly of primary sources in Greek and Latin, on the Greco-Roman world just before and after the time of Christ. He also had many authoritative works of the early Church Fathers.

Under "Moral Philosophy" Jefferson had the original works

of his favorite Stoic and Epicurean philosophers as well as the English, Scotch, and American deistic writers that so much influenced his own philosophical and religious beliefs. Here, too, he had many of the French atheists of his own acquaintance, who, his writings reveal, did not influence him as much as his enemies believed.[182]

Under the topic of "Law of Nature and Nations," which Jefferson regarded as a branch of ethics, since the same moral law that guided the moral beliefs of individuals and moral philosophers could also be seen in nature and behind the laws of nations, Jefferson had the fundamental authorities on the moral basis of law and society, and the important Enlightenment writers. These many works, which might be missed entirely in considering Jefferson's religious collection, indicate clearly the strongly intellectual, moral, and studious nature of Jefferson's religion, and that he had made a thorough study of religion from the Enlightenment point of view, even going to primary sources.

This same scholarly interest is indicated by Jefferson's extensive collection of Bibles, New Testaments, individual books of the Bible, and works of the Apocrypha in Greek, Latin, English, and French. He also had numerous reference works to aid in studying the Bible, including concordances, harmonies, maps, and commentaries on the Enlightenment interpretation by Priestley and others.

Jefferson's interest in religious devotions is revealed by the many works he had not only of Anglican prayer books, books of worship, and rules and beliefs of the church, but of Catholic "Books of Hours," and meditations for dissenters. Jefferson also had a collection of *Catechisms* and books on festival and fast days.

Although theology was by Jefferson's own admission not his favorite topic of religious discussion, he did have a wide variety of works on theology ranging from the original works of Calvin, with whom Jefferson violently disagreed, to small tracts by many authors of many sects. With a fine impartiality, Jefferson had collected works attacking and defending Catholicism and different Protestant beliefs. He had both long and short studies on typical Christian theological doctrines from salvation to the resurrection.

[140]

Jefferson also had an unexpectedly large collection of sermons, ranging from short tracts to long serious works of up to eighteen volumes. The books represented clergymen of a wide spectrum of churches and faiths and covered a variety of topics from theological doctrine and denominational beliefs to topics of current religious and patriotic interest. He also had tracts and reports of many religious organizations in his library.

Under the classification "Ecclesiastical Law" and "Common Law," Jefferson had a group of basic law books that he used not only for study of law but in studying the problem of religious freedom and the establishment of the church. Although he did have a few titles on the subject of religious freedom, it is plain that Jefferson based his extensive study and writing on the subject of religious freedom more on these original sources in canon and civil law than on secondary opinions of contemporaries. The writings of Milton and Locke were important influences upon Jefferson's ideas of religious freedom.

Jefferson also had many varied works on morals, manners, and the duties of ladies and gentlemen. Such works of a past age were congenial to his beliefs concerning the importance of courtesy and morality in society.

To summarize, scattered in various subject classifications Jefferson had a more extensive collection of materials on religion and ethics than many people have realized. He had more works on theology and a larger collection of sermons than his own critical comments on those topics have led investigators to suppose. Although not forming as large a proportion of his total library as in many of the libraries of his contemporaries, numerically his collection of homiletics and theology was larger than most. It was characterized by fairness and impartiality in presenting many points of view. Jefferson's collection of devotional works and books of catechism reveal a religious interest that has often been overlooked.

He had an extensive collection of the works of the moral philosophers of the Enlightenment and of the classical age, to which he often referred in his writings, indicating the ethical and deistic emphasis of his religion. Priestley and Middleton were most important, he said, in influencing his belief in one Creator God and in Jesus Christ as the greatest of moral teachers.[183]

The many titles on church law and on the moral foundations of all law in his extensive law collection is another indication of Jefferson's strong ethical emphasis, which is supported by his writings on political and social theory. He saw law as a reflection of the moral code rooted in man's conscience by God, and he based this belief on his reading and study of such authors as Kames, Helvetius, Hobbes, and Wollaston, he wrote to a friend.[184]

Another unexpected religious interest of Jefferson which is indicated by his library collection is his scholarly interest in studying the Bible and the early days of Christianity. His extensive collection of Bibles in original languages, his many tools for research, such as concordances and harmonies, as well as his collection of the works by the early Church Fathers and of early church history, indicate his interest in studying the beliefs of the first "primitive" Christians, an interest which he shared with liberal ministers and friends with whom he corresponded. Jefferson's library collection on religious and ethical subjects reveals that, although he was more liberal in his religious convictions than some, but not all, of his contemporaries, he was not only not opposed to religion, as some of his critics accused him of being,[185] but was a deeply religious and ethical person, as he himself stated to his close friends.[186]

A careful study of the titles in the religious and ethical sections of Jefferson's library gives important clues, then, to the understanding of particular religious beliefs which have sometimes puzzled scholars. When Jefferson's statements about his reading interests and the important books that stimulated his thinking are considered, along with the extensive notes he made, his many scattered references to his own strongly held convictions are far more understandable than when considered by themselves. Such a study of his religious library leads the student to the inevitable conclusion that Jefferson's liberal Unitarian idea of God as the great Creator of material man and his universe and of Jesus Christ as, not the Son of God, but the greatest teacher of morals who ever lived, was the result of his study of congenial Enlightenment authors such as Lord Bolingbroke, and of contemporary liberal preachers such as Joseph Priestley. Jefferson's religious writings need to be placed in the setting of contemporary thought in order not to be misunderstood today.

It would well repay Jeffersonian scholars to study other aspects of his library and reading habits in some detail to understand his many other interests and those aspects of his complex character and thought that have puzzled modern historians. The bibliographical mode of historical research offers, in addition, important advantages for understanding the inner life of thought and belief for other important Presidents and world leaders of literary inclination.

5

Conclusions

DESPITE THE MANY studies that have been made of the life and thought of Thomas Jefferson, comparatively little research has been done on the library and literary interests of Jefferson. The nature of Jefferson's library and its history has been well documented but the extent and the nature of Jefferson's library activities, his philosophy of librarianship, and the implications of the reading interests revealed by the works in his library have been neglected.

The Importance of Library History

Although it has been recognized that libraries contain a record of the important ideas and forces that have shaped men's lives and their societies and are intellectual forces affecting social change, too few studies have been made by scholars using this important resource for historical and biographical research. The primary source materials of influential books and the reading interests which they imply become increasingly important the farther the researcher is removed from the period he is studying. By studying the intellectual life of important historical people such as Thomas Jefferson as revealed in their libraries and writings, new insight may be gained concerning many of the contradictions of character and beliefs that have puzzled

[144]

holdings, interpreted in the light of his own comprehensive writings and comments, can lead to a better understanding of the nature and source of Jefferson's most important beliefs about man, society, and religion, which so greatly influenced his ideas and actions. As William Peden wrote at the conclusion of his study of Jefferson's libraries:

> The Jeffersonian library catalogues, . . . coupled with Jefferson's innumerable . . . writings, enable us to reconstruct the reading habits, the likes and dislikes, the critical opinions, the prejudices and predilections of one of our greatest men. Together, they furnish us with an invaluable index not only to the mind and character of Thomas Jefferson, but to the tumultuous period in which he lived and played his uncalculably important role.[1]

Indications of Jefferson's Nature and Interests from the Characteristics of His Library

The time, expense, thought, and care that Jefferson lavished on his library all his life is an indication of the importance that he placed upon reading, study, and the library skills that facilitate study. He said that he had a "canine appetite for reading,"[2] and that he was a "hard student" when young and again when "retired . . . at the age of seventy-six."[3] Books were essential for an educated person, he believed, and, writing to a father concerning his son's education and recommending a list of books to be purchased, he said, "A lawyer without books would be like a workman without tools."[4] So essential to Jefferson was reading that he formed a small traveling library composed of compact editions to take with him on his travels.[5] After he sold the main library that he had spent his lifetime collecting to the United States Congress to replace their library which had been destroyed when the British burned the Capitol during the War of 1812, Jefferson could not forbear from collecting another, smaller library for his studies, although he was then past seventy, saying, "I cannot live without books."[6] Jefferson's main library at Monticello, which he wrote he had "been fifty years making . . . and . . . spared no pains, opportunity or expense," grew to "between nine and ten thousand volumes."[7]

Jefferson had diligently ordered books from the leading book sellers of America, England, and Europe. "While residing in Paris," he wrote, "I devoted every afternoon . . . in examining all the principal bookstores."[8]

A close study of Jefferson's library, as made by E. Millicent Sowerby,[9] reveals that he was most meticulous about the care and arrangement of his library, carrying on all the important librarian functions necessary for the use and control of the library. He inspected and collated each book as it arrived, initialing the signatures and marking each work with its shelf position number. He developed a detailed classification system for the works of his library based on the "Tables of Sciences" by which Lord Bacon classified human knowledge,[10] which was used by the library of the University of Virginia and became the basis of the Library of Congress classification system.[11] Jefferson methodically kept a book catalog to facilitate the use of his library both by subject and author classification. He was generous in lending books to his friends but kept records of his loans. In planning the library for the University of Virginia he developed detailed rules of circulation. Throughout his life, Jefferson provided expert reading advice to many friends, neighbors, and family members from his wide knowledge of books and authors.

A study of the contents of Jefferson's library, when coupled with his own statements about his literary interests, tells a good deal about the interests, character, and beliefs of Thomas Jefferson. Jefferson is revealed as being unusually studious all his life, continuing and enlarging the mental stimulation and intellectual activities that his college teachers exposed him to as a youth. While his library gives evidence of his extraordinary and continuing study of the profession of law, and even more evidence of his study of political and social science as a statesman, it also reveals a wide range of other interests, such as art, science, and literature. Jefferson was far from provincial in his outlook and had wider cultural interests than his contemporaries. He was not, however, of artistic or imaginative temperament. He enjoyed performing music but not composing it. In art, his interest was architecture and in literature his taste ran to serious nonfictional works rather than fictional ones. The classical poets and dramatists, of which Jefferson was very fond, were the exceptions.

For all his aristocratic tastes, Jefferson's library shows that he had a practical interest in farming, invention, and small industry flowing from his needs as a plantation owner. The exceptionally large number of scientific works in his library is an indication of Jefferson's keen interest in science, especially natural science. The fact that he lived in one of the less settled regions of Virginia and knew and admired local Indian tribes gave Jefferson a lifelong interest in the American natural habitat and the frontier.

Jefferson also owed his interest in science to his admiration for the studies of Newton, Bacon, and Locke. Scientific progress and the development of reason and learning promised great advancement for human freedom and happiness, especially in America where natural resources were abundant and human hopes had not been stifled by centuries of oppression. Writing to John Adams, Jefferson expressed the conviction that science indicated "how much is still ahead . . . unexplained and unexplored," even though scientific advancement had brought them to a "Place . . . as far before our ancestors, as in the rear of our posterity."[12]

Jefferson's continuing studies of the Enlightenment and of the philosophy of the rights of man reinforced democratic tendencies gained from his interest in the American frontier. The result gave Jefferson a liberal political and social point of view unusual in men of his class, and led him to use his studies and talents to become the most important leader for Enlightenment progress of his time. Reflecting on the oppressions of the Napoleonic wars Jefferson wrote, near the end of his life:

> Yet I will not believe our labors are lost. I shall not die without a hope that light and liberty are on a steady advance. . . . The art of printing alone, and the vast dissemination of books, will maintain the mind where it is. . . . And even should the cloud of barbarism and despotism again obscure the science and liberties of Europe, this country remains to preserve and restore the light and liberty to them. In short, the flames kindled on the 4th. of July

1776. have spread over too much of the globe to be extinguished by the feeble engines of despotism. On the contrary they will consume those engines, and all who work them.[13]

The comparison of Jefferson's library with other contemporary libraries indicates that his interests were more in accord with those of the college professors of his time than with those of the common people, an impression that is supported by the many letters Jefferson wrote on intellectual subjects to friends who were college professors, ministers, and doctors. Jefferson's lack of interest in fiction, light literature, and popular biography indicates his essentially intellectual and serious tastes.

The picture of Jefferson that emerges from a study of his library is of a very intelligent, intellectual, and studious person of many interests who distrusted emotion and imagination and kept his own feelings tightly under control except when with family and close friends. His ability and industry made him one of the most influential leaders of his time both over the minds and the lives of men. His library reflects his talents and his industry.

Indications of Jefferson's Religious Beliefs from the Characteristics of His Library Collection on Religion and Ethics

When Jefferson's library holdings are carefully scrutinized for titles of a religious nature, especially when the differences in subject classification used by Jefferson and those practiced today are taken into account, his library collection on religious subjects is found to be more extensive than many investigators have realized. Although Jefferson did not maintain that religion was one of the major emphases of his library, careful research indicates that Jefferson had made considerable studies of religious and moral subjects and that his library holdings on religion, ethics, moral philosophy, church history, ecclesiastical law, the moral philosophy of law and society, Biblical studies, devotional material, modern sects and cults, and religious societies were extensive. It seems evident that scholars have been misled by the relatively small proportion of Jefferson's library classified as "theological" in comparison with other contemporary libraries which were not as finely classified as Jefferson's, and by Jefferson's expressed aversion to the subject of "theological disputation."

Despite his own feelings, Jefferson did have a large section in his library on works of theological argument on a wide variety of topics from many points of view, as well as an extensive collection of sermons by clergymen of many backgrounds. This diversity reflects Jefferson's own broad-mindedness and his librarian's appreciation of the importance of preserving all sorts of materials. He similarly had a fine collection of the writings of Calvin, although he often expressed strong disapproval of Calvin's theology.[14] Jefferson studied thoroughly authors whose beliefs he opposed as well as those with whom he agreed.

Both Jefferson's writings and his religious library holdings document his opposition to Calvinism, Puritanism, and the narrow New England religion of "revelation," in contrast with the liberal religion of "reason" which he had come to admire from his study of Enlightenment authors such as Lord Bolingbroke. Jefferson's library is filled with the works of the Enlightenment deistic philosophers and Unitarian ministers who influenced his religion, and gives clear indication of his liberal emphasis. Yet Jefferson was not the "atheist, deist, or devil" which he said his enemies accused him of being.[15] He believed in God ruling His creation by moral law which his readings in Newton, Bacon, Kames, and Helvetius had suggested. It is possible to trace his religious and intellectual development by the authors he mentions, as when he wrote to Adams:

> I think that every Christian sect . . . of Calvin gives a great handle to Atheism . . . [and] the disciples of Ocellus, Timaeus, Spinosa, Diderot and D'Holbach . . . by their general dogma that without a revelation, there would not be sufficient proof of the being of a god. . . . On the contrary I hold (without appeal to revelation) that when we take a view of the Universe, . . . it is impossible . . . for the human mind not to believe that there is, . . . design, cause and effect, up to an ultimate cause, a fabricator of all things from matter and motion, their preserver and regulator . . . and . . . superintending power.[16]

Jefferson also was led by his studies of Milton and Locke to believe in the God-given rights of man, especially the right to religious freedom. Besides the works in his library on religious freedom, Jefferson used his extensive collection of titles on early church history and heresies,[17] as well as his legal authors on the origins of civil, common, and ecclesiastical law and his collection of authorities on the moral basis of law in society, for his own extensive studies and writings on religious freedom and the separation of church and state.

Jefferson's writings on ethics and morality indicate that he used works from his library on law and moral philosophy to support his own belief in the importance of morality for man. Not only was the world of nature designed and governed by a good Fabricator for the welfare of mankind, Jefferson expounded from his studies, but the society of man was governed by the moral law for the good of all.[18] All people and all society, men, rulers, and nations, had moral rights and moral duties to follow. This was the basis of law, government, ethics, and religion for Jefferson, and his well-used library bears witness. Further indication of the importance for Jefferson of writings on morality is seen in the section he had in his library on the moral problem of slavery and the section on the proper morals and manners for "the lady and gentleman." Ever the courteous gentleman, Jefferson saw manners and courtesy as the everyday practice of the larger morality he advocated for political reform.

Jefferson's lack of philosophical and mystical works in his library collection under "Religion" reflects his practical and scientific bent of mind, although he did have the works of Plato, whom he criticized as being too abstract and mystical.[19] There was, however, an unexpectedly large section in Jefferson's library of devotional material from all denominations, reflecting an interest in private devotions, which Jefferson practiced regularly.[20] This interest probably came from Jefferson's long exposure to the worship of the Episcopalian church.[21]

Another religious interest of Jefferson, revealed by his library holdings, is his interest, shared with other men of the Enlightenment, in studying and comparing different religions. Jefferson wrote to like-minded friends of his interest in comparing the moral teachings of Jesus Christ with great moralists of the past, such as Socrates, Seneca, and Epicurus.[22] After he had made such a comparison in outline form, Jefferson wrote of Jesus' teachings, "A system of morals is presented to us, which, if filled up in the style and spirit of the rich fragments he left us, would be the most perfect and sublime that has ever been taught by man," indicating the conviction resulting from his studies.[23]

Jefferson wrote to Adams concerning the works in his library that he had used for his study of comparative religion. He mentioned "Enfield's judicious abridgment of Brucker's *History of Philosophy*, in which he has reduced five or six quarto volumes of the thousand pages each of Latin closely printed to two moderate octavos of English open type."[24] It is also evident that Jefferson used his copies of the classical moralists as well in this study.

Jefferson also had the Enlightenment enthusiasm for stripping away the later superstitions of the medieval church and getting back to the pure "primitive" teachings of Christ. He wrote of studying the New Testament for such a purpose and did make his own versions of Jesus' life and teachings from the Gospel accounts.[25] Jefferson's large collection of works by the early Church fathers and historians in original languages is evidence of this scholarly interest. Jefferson also used the many language versions of the Bible and New Testament, as well as the commentaries, concordances, and harmonies of the Bible in his library collection for these studies.

One result of a study of Jefferson's library which has not been heretofore recognized by Jefferson scholars is the realization that his classical studies equipped him to be a fine Biblical scholar. His extensive collection of Bibles and New Testaments in original languages, along with the many tools for Biblical study and research which he possessed and used, could be duplicated only by the theological seminary libraries. It is not surprising that a "Bible" was one of the few books Jefferson wrote. It is only surprising that the keen religious interests of this great, but reticent, American have gone unrecognized for so long.

The Private Faith of a Bibliophile

A study of Jefferson's reading interests and library activities shows him to be a confirmed bibliophile in the broadest sense of the word. He loved books and libraries and he knew them well. He understood the processes of printing and the book trade and appreciated a well-made book. As a good scholar, he knew the importance of well-written and documented works for transmitting information. He realized and used the vast resources of information and inspiration of the past, recorded in books. He also understood the importance of gathering and organizing books into libraries so that their information would be readily available, and was concerned with the deeper issues of librarianship, such as preventing the censorship of books and the destruction of libraries. Peden concluded from his study of Jefferson as book collector:

> It can be seen, then, that as a librarian whose method of book classification was in active use for almost a century, Jefferson again was a man ahead of his time; and that as an encourager of American book publication and as an apostle of dissemination of the great ideas and messages preserved in the written word he was a man whose influence upon the growing nation, which he himself had struggled to foster and preserve, is virtually incalculable.[26]

It is plain from Jefferson's life and writings that he was one of those few individuals to whom books were more than objects and a library more than a place. Books, in the hands of his college teachers, were the means by which the wisdom of the past and the exciting advances of the present were opened up to him. Books were the tools of his profession and the sources for the answers to the problems of daily living, from how to court a wife or build a house to how to meet the sorrow of death or guide a nation. From his studies in his library, Jefferson gained his understanding of the world and life, and his interpretation of religion and the universe. His reading gave Jefferson not only a hope for a better life for mankind and a dazzling vision of America's future, but also the means for working for those goals. After his retirement from the political struggle, books became for him the consolation of his old age and familiar friends who never betrayed him. Jefferson was, indeed, a lover of books.

The study of Jefferson's books, particularly of those with great ideas that gripped his mind, is especially rewarding because of their influence upon Jefferson's thought and life, and, through him, upon American history. Peden writes:

> Jefferson was . . . an innovator and a trail-blazer. A study of his libraries not only adds to our knowledge of the age in which Jefferson lived, but throws light on the man who, more aptly than any other American, can be called the Leonardo of the New World.[27]

The realization of the importance to his thought and action of Jefferson's wide reading in many fields suggests important comparisons with other American presidents and world leaders of similar wide intellectual interests. Peterson comments that President John F. Kennedy, another Renaissance man, in a dinner honoring the Nobel laureates of the Americas, called his guests "the most extraordinary collection of talents . . . that has ever been gathered together at the White House, with the possible exception of when Thomas Jefferson dined alone."[28]

Indeed, with the advances in historical research that have made us aware of the complicated interplay of events, both good and bad, in the flow of history and with the advances in psychology that have made us aware of the complicated motives, both good and evil, of those people who affected history, the study of the inner lives of men becomes ever more important. More studies of the reading and thinking of historical figures such as Jefferson and of world leaders of the present need to be undertaken in order to understand the beliefs and actions of such men who have affected the lives of us all. This type of study is particularly important for people of complexity, such as Jefferson, and for matters easily misunderstood, such as religion. It is unfortunate that few studies of the intellectual and spiritual lives of our great leaders have been made. Peterson emphasizes this need in writing of Jefferson:

> None of the ordinary categories of the hero—lawgiver, chieftain, prophet—sufficed for Jefferson. As his character was somewhat labyrinthian, so his mind was bewildering in its range and complexity. Later generations comprehended his thought only in fragments.[29]

Jefferson, moreover, not only was actively engaged in the great issues of American life during his own lifetime, but also anticipated the bewildering issues of America's future. As Peterson comments, Jefferson "with Adams summed up an epoch; but Jefferson—his ideas and ideals, his prophecies and legacies—was engaged in the great campaigns of history to come."[30]

Research on Jefferson's studies and life strongly indicate what one person of ability and diligence can accomplish to overcome great human problems. If modern social problems are more complicated than in Jefferson's world, so the accumulated resources of human knowledge and wisdom available in libraries are more expansive and accessible. Perhaps we need today more of Jefferson's zeal in seeking and accumulating answers to our problems from library sources. If so, a study of Jefferson's example is instructive to people today.

Notes

Notes to Preface

1. Julian P. Boyd, ed., *The Papers of Thomas Jefferson* 17 vols. (Princeton: Princeton University Press, 1950-65).

2. M. Rosaleen Trainor, "Thomas Jefferson on Freedom of Conscience" (Ph.D. dissertation, St. John's University, 1966); Constance Bartlett Schulz, "The Radical Religious Ideas of Thomas Jefferson and John Adams: A Comparison" (Ph.D. dissertation, University of Cincinnati, 1973); Kenneth Raynor Williams, "The Ethics of Thomas Jefferson" (Ph.D. dissertation, Boston University, 1962); Reginald Charles Stuart, "Encounter with Mars: Thomas Jefferson's View of War" (Ph.D. dissertation, University of Florida, 1974); Burton Spivak, "Jefferson, England, and the Embargo" (Ph.D. dissertation, University of Virginia, 1975).

3. William Harwood Peden, "Thomas Jefferson: Book-Collector" (Ph.D. dissertation, University of Virginia, 1942); James Albert Servies, "Thomas Jefferson and His Bibliographic Classification" (Master's thesis, University of Chicago, 1950).

4. *Dissertation Abstracts International*, "Retrospective Index," 8 (1970); *Comprehensive Dissertation Index, 1861-1972*, "Library Science," 31, "Humanities and Social Sciences," 33; *Dissertation Abstracts International*, "Humanities and Social Sciences," (June-December, 1973), 34 (January-December, 1974), 35 (January-April, 1975).

Notes to Chapter 1

1. Stanley Pargellis, "Long Life to the Library History Round Table," *American Library History Reader*, ed. by John David Marshall (Hamden, Conn.: Shoe String Press, 1961), pp. 8, 9.

2. Ibid., p. 10.

3. Louis Shores, "Importance of Library History," *American Library History Reader*, ed. by John David Marshall (Hamden, Conn.: Shoe String Press, 1961), pp. 4-5.

4. Austin Baxter Keep, *The Library of Colonial New York* (New York: Burt Franklin, 1970).

5. Jesse H. Shera, *Foundations of the Public Library: The Origins of the Public Library Movement in New England 1629-1855* (Hamden, Conn.: Shoe String Press, 1965), p. 248. (Hereafter referred to as *Public Library*.)

6. James D. Hart, *The Popular Book; a History of America's Literary Taste* (New York: Oxford Press, 1950), p. 12.

7. Shera, *Public Library*, p. 248.

8. Ibid., p. 248.

9. Samuel Elliot Morrison, *The Intellectual Life of Colonial New England* (Ithaca, N.Y.: Cornell University Press, 1965). (Hereafter referred to as *Intellectual Life of New England*.)

10. Elmer Johnson, *History of Libraries in the Western World*, 2d ed. (Metuchen, N.J.: Scarecrow Press, 1970), p. 324. (Hereafter referred to as *History of Libraries*.)

Notes to Chapter 2

1. See James Albert Servies, "Thomas Jefferson and His Bibliographic Classification" (Master's thesis, University of Chicago, 1950) (hereafter cited as "Bibliographic Classification") and William Harwood Peden, "Thomas Jefferson: Book-Collector" (Ph.D. dissertation, University of Virginia, 1942) (hereafter cited as "Book-Collector") and E. Millicent Sowerby, comp., *Catalogue of the Library of Thomas Jefferson*, 5 vols. (Washington, D.C.: Library of Congress, 1952-59) (hereafter cited as *Catalogue*).

2. See William Peden, "Some Notes on Jefferson's Libraries," *William and Mary Quarterly*, 3rd series 1 (July, 1944); Randolph Greenfield Adams, *Three Americanists: Henry Harrisse, Bibliographer, George Brinley, Book Collector, Thomas Jefferson, Librarian* (Philadelphia: University of Pennsylvania Press, 1939) (hereafter cited as *Librarian*). Arthur Bestor, "Thomas Jefferson and the Freedom of Books," *Three Presidents and Their Books* (Urbana, Ill.: University of Illinois Press, 1955).

3. Henry Stephens Randall, *The Life of Thomas Jefferson*, 3 vols. (New York: Derby and Jackson, 1858), 3:407-10 (hereafter cited as *Life*); Dumas Malone, *Jefferson and His Time*, Vol. 1: *Jefferson the Virginian* (Boston: Little, Brown and Co., 1948), pp. 401-402, (hereafter cited as *Jefferson the Virginian*); Karl Lehmann, *Thomas Jefferson: American Humanist* (Chicago: University of Chicago Press, 1965), pp. 16-22, (hereafter cited as *American Humanist*): Adrienne Koch, *The Philosophy of Thomas Jefferson* (Gloucester, Mass.: Peter Smith, 1957), pp. 47-48, 105-108 (hereafter cited as *Philosophy*).

4. Gilbert Chinard, ed., *The Literary Bible of Thomas Jefferson: His Commonplace Book of Philosophers and Poets* (New York: Greenwood Press, 1969), pp. 8-15, 23-29. (Hereafter referred to as *Literary Bible.*)

5. Jefferson wrote that the only purpose of reading fiction was that "The field of imagination is thus laid open to our use and lessons may be formed to illustrate . . . every moral rule of life," Jefferson to Robert Skipwith, 3 August 1771, Albert Ellery Bergh, ed., *The Writings of Thomas Jefferson*, 20 vols. (Washington, D.C.: The Thomas Jefferson Memorial Association, 1907), 4:239. (Hereafter referred to as *Writings.*)

6. Jefferson, *Autobiography*, Bergh, *Writings*, 1:3.

7. Jefferson to Dr. Thomas Cooper, 10 February 1814, Bergh, *Writings*, 14:85.

8. Jefferson, *Education for a Lawyer*, 1767, Saul K. Padover, ed., *The Complete Jefferson* (New York: Duel, Sloan, and Pearce, 1943), pp. 1043-47. (Hereafter referred to as *Complete Jefferson.*)

9. Lehmann, *American Humanist*, p. 14.

10. Jefferson to Dr. Joseph Priestley, 27 January 1800, Bergh, *Writings*, 10:146-47.

11. Jefferson to John Brazier, 24 August 1819, ibid., 15:208.

12. Ibid., p. 209.

13. Isaac Jefferson, *Memoirs of a Monticello Slave* (Charlottesville, Va.: University of Virginia Press, 1951), pp. 27-28, in Malone, *Jefferson the Virginian*, p. 402.

14. Chastellux, Francois Jean, Marquis dè, *Travels in North-America in the Years 1780, 1781, 1782*, trans. G. Grieve, 2 vols. (Dublin: printed for Colles, Moncrieffe, White, H. Whitestone, Byrne, Cash, Marchbank, Henry, and Moore, 1787), 2:45, in Malone, *Jefferson the Virginian*, p. 392, and Chinard, *Literary Bible*, pp. 25-26.

15. Malone, *Jefferson the Virginian*, p. 402.

16. Jefferson to Samuel Harrison Smith, 21 September 1814, Bergh, *Writings*, 14:191.

17. Jefferson to William Short, 31 October 1819, ibid., 15:221.

18. Randall, *Life*, 3:350.

19. Jefferson to Dr. Vine Utley, 21 March 1819, Bergh, *Writings*, 15:187-88.

20. Jefferson to Charles Thomson, 9 January 1816, ibid., 14:386-87.

21. Jefferson to Dr. Benjamin Waterhouse, 3 March 1818, ibid., 15:164.

22. Randall, *Life*, 3:346.

23. Jefferson to Adams, 1 June 1822, Lester J. Cappon, ed., *The Adams-Jefferson Letters*, 2 vols. (Chapel Hill, N.C.: University of North Carolina Press, 1959), 2:578. (Hereafter referred to as *Adams-Jefferson Letters.*)

24. Jefferson to Adams, 17 May 1818, ibid., p. 524. Note that Jefferson's own spelling is generally followed in his quotations.

25. Jefferson to Adams, 14 October 1816, ibid., p. 491.

26. Ibid.

27. Ibid.

28. Such a request led to Jefferson's discussing several works on the origin of the American Indians: Jefferson to Adams, 11 June 1812, ibid., pp. 305-308.

29. Jefferson to Abigail Adams, 22 August 1813, ibid., pp. 366-67.

30. Jefferson to Edward Livingston, 4 April 1824, Bergh, *Writings*, 16:25-26.

31. Jefferson to William Short, 31 October 1819, ibid., 15:221.

32. Jefferson to John Brazier, 24 August 1819, ibid., p. 209.

33. Randall, *Life*, 3:350.

34. Jefferson, *Autobiography*, Bergh *Writings*, 1:3-4.

35. Lehmann, *American Humanist*, p. 11.

36. John Fitzgerald to Jefferson, 1 April 1781, Julian P. Boyd, ed., *The Papers of Thomas Jefferson* (Princeton: Princeton University Press, 1950-65), 5:311-12. (Hereafter referred to as *Papers*.)

37. Jefferson to John Page, 21 February 1770, Bergh, *Writings*, 4:18.

38. See Sowerby, *Catalogue*, where she has cited and quoted all available bibliographic information and references to ordering each of the books in Jefferson's main library from Jefferson's letters.

39. Jefferson to John Randolph, 25 August 1775, Boyd, *Papers*, 1:242-43.

40. Jefferson to Ebenezer Hazard, 30 April 1775, ibid., p. 164, n., p. 165.

41. Jefferson to Madison, 20 February 1784, ibid., 6:554.

42. John Stockdale to Jefferson, 12 August 1785, ibid., 8:365.

43. Jefferson to John Stockdale 24 July 1786, ibid., 10:165-66.

44. Jefferson to William Stephens Smith 13 September 1786, ibid., pp. 362-63.

45. Jefferson to Samuel H. Smith, 21 September 1814, Bergh, *Writings*, 14:191.

46. Ibid.

47. William Carmichael to Jefferson, 17 December 1785, Boyd, *Papers*, 9:105.

48. Jefferson to Van Damme, 18 March 1788, ibid., 12:678-79.

49. Madison to Jefferson, 27 April 1785, ibid., 8:111.

50. Jefferson to Madison, 1 September 1785, ibid., pp. 460-64.

51. Jefferson to Andre Limozin, 11 September 1785, 28 September 1785, ibid., pp. 513, 565.

52. Jefferson to Madison, 2 August 1787, ibid., 11:662.

53. Jefferson to Alexander Donald, 7 February 1788, ibid., 12:571.

54. Jefferson to Charles Bellini, 3 September 1785, Bergh, *Writings*, 5:152-53.

55. Jefferson to Martha Jefferson Randolph, 8 May 1791, Edwin Morris Betts and James Adam Bear, Jr., eds., *The Family Letters of Thomas Jefferson* (Columbia, Mo.: University of Missouri Press, 1966), pp. 80-81. (Hereafter referred to as *Family Letters*.)

56. Jefferson to Thomas Jefferson Randolph, 21 February 1803, ibid., p. 242.

57. Thomas Jefferson Randolph to Jefferson, 24 February 1803, ibid., p. 243.

58. Jefferson to Madison, 1 September 1785, Boyd, *Papers*, 8:450-64.

59. Jefferson to Madison, 2 August 1787, ibid., 11:662-63.

60. Jefferson to Robert Skipwith, 3 August 1771, ibid., 1:76-81.

61. Peden, "Book-Collector," p. 89.

62. Adrienne Koch, *Jefferson and Madison* (New York: Aldred A. Knopf, 1950), pp. 19, 23-31.

63. Ibid., p. 16.

64. Jefferson to Franklin, to Adams, and to Jay, 5 October 1781, Boyd, *Papers*, 6:126.

65. Jefferson to Monroe, 5 October 1781, ibid., p. 127.

66. Monroe to Jefferson, 9 September 1780, ibid., 3:622.

67. Jefferson to Thomas Turpin, 5 February 1769, ibid., 1:23-24.

68. Jefferson to Martha Jefferson, 28 March 1787, Betts, *Family Letters*, pp. 34-36.

69. Jefferson to Peter Carr, 19 August 1785, Boyd, *Papers*, 8:405-12.

70. Jefferson to Peter Carr, 10 August 1787, ibid., 12:14-19.

71. Francis Wayles Eppes to Jefferson, 22 March 1822, Betts, *Family Letters*, pp. 442-43.

72. Jefferson to Francis Wayles Eppes, 9 April 1822, ibid., pp. 443-45.

73. Jefferson to Gen. Thaddeus Kosciusko, 26 February 1810, Bergh, *Writings*, 12:369.

74. Jefferson to Dabney Terrell, 26 February 1821, Jefferson to Dr. Thomas Cooper, 16 January 1814, Padover, *Complete Jefferson*, pp. 1088-90.

75. Jefferson to John Brazier, 24 August 1819, ibid., pp. 1086-88.

76. Jefferson to an unnamed member of University of Virginia faculty, 25 October 1824, ibid., pp. 1094-96.

77. Jefferson to Nathaniel Burwell, 14 March 1818, Bergh, *Writings*, 15:165.

78. Ibid., pp. 166-68.

79. Ibid., p. 165.

80. Jefferson to Martha Jefferson, 28 November 1783, Betts, *Family Letters*, pp. 19, 20, n. 1.

81. Ibid., p. 19. Jefferson's spelling and eighteenth century grammatical customs are followed in all quotations.

82. Jefferson to Nathaniel Burwell, 14 March 1818, Bergh, *Writings*, 15:166.

83. See Roy J. Honeywell, *The Educational Work of Thomas Jefferson* (New York: Russell and Russell, 1964). (Hereafter referred to as *Educational Work.*)

84. See Jefferson, Bill for More General Diffusion of Knowledge, Boyd, *Papers*, 2:526-33, n.s. pp. 534-35.

85. Jefferson, *Autobiography*, Paul Leicester Ford, ed., *The Writings of Thomas Jefferson*, 10 vols. (New York: G. P. Putnam's Sons, 1892-98), 1:66. (Hereafter referred to as *Writings.*)

86. Honeywell, *Educational Work*, p. 67.

87. Ford, *Writings*, 1:67.
88. Jefferson to George Wythe, 13 August 1786, Bergh, *Writings*, 5:397.
89. Jefferson to La Fayette, 14 May 1817, ibid., 15:116.
90. Jefferson to Dupont de Nemours, 24 April 1816, ibid., 14:491-92.
91. Jefferson, *Thoughts on Lotteries*, February, 1826, Bergh, *Writings*, 17:462.
92. Jefferson, *Report of the Commissioners of the University of Virginia*, August 1-4, 1818, Padover, *Complete Jefferson*, pp. 1097-98.
93. Jefferson to Gen. Thaddeus Kosciusko, 26 February 1810, Bergh, *Writings*, 12:369-70.
94. Jefferson to Ira H. Taylor, Benjamin F. Nourse and John C. Tidball, 8 March 1824, Saul K. Padover, ed., *A Jefferson Profile* (New York: John Day Co., 1956), p. 334. (Hereafter referred to as *Jefferson Profile*.)
95. See Malone, *Jefferson the Virginian*, p. 285; Lehmann, *American Humanist*, p. 204; Henry Wilder Foote, *Thomas Jefferson: Champion of Religious Freedom, Advocate of Christian Morals* (Boston: Beacon Press, 1947), p. 16. (Hereafter referred to as *Champion, Advocate*.)
96. Jefferson, "A Bill for Establishing a Public Library," Boyd, *Papers*, 2:544.
97. Jefferson, *Notes on Virginia*, Query 14, Ford, *Writings*, 3:255.
98. Boyd, *Papers*, 2:544-45, n. 1.
99. Jefferson, "A Bill for Establishing a Public Library," ibid., p. 544.
100. "Report of a Committee to Prepare a List of Books for Congress," 24 January 1783, Boyd, *Papers*, 6:216.
101. Jefferson to John Wyche, 19 May 1809, Bergh, *Writings*, 12:282.
102. See Merrill D. Peterson, *Thomas Jefferson and the New Nation* (New York: Oxford University Press, 1970), p. 27 (Hereafter referred to as *New Nation*); Norman Cousins, *In God We Trust: the Religious Beliefs and Ideas of the American Founding Fathers* (New York: Harper Brothers, 1958), pp. 114-15 (Hereafter referred to as *In God We Trust*.)
103. Lehmann, *American Humanist*, p. 16.
104. Ibid.
105. Malone, *Jefferson the Virginian*, p. 127.
106. Jefferson, *Account Book for 1773*, in ibid.
107. Jefferson, *Diary*, quoted in Thomas Jefferson, *The Commonplace Book of Thomas Jefferson: A Repertory of His Ideas on Government*, ed. Gilbert Chinard (Baltimore: Johns Hopkins Press, 1926), p. 2. (Hereafter referred to as *Commonplace Book*.)
108. Malone, *Jefferson the Virginian*, p. 401, citing Peden, "Book-Collector," chap. 8. Peden, indeed, has studied in detail old records of Jefferson's book purchases for his first library of college books purchased from the book publisher of the *Virginia Gazette* newspaper in Williamsburg, as well as his purchases for his "Great Library" in America and Europe, his purchases for his "Last Library" after he sold his library to Congress, and his purchases for the library of the University of Virginia; Peden, "Book-Collector," pp. 96-98, 103-108, 113-24, 126-39, 156-65, 168-79.

109. Peterson, *New Nation*, pp. 265-66.

110. Malone, *Jefferson the Virginian*, p. 401, citing Thomas Jefferson, "Library Catalogue," in the Massachusetts Historical Society collection.

111. Jefferson to Dr. Thomas Cooper, 16 January 1814, Bergh, *Writings*, 14:60.

112. Jefferson to Samuel H. Smith, 21 September 1814, ibid., pp. 191-92.

113. Chastellux, Francois Jean, Marquis de, *Travels in North-America in the Years 1780-81-82* (New York: n.p., 1827), p. 81, quoted in Adrieℓne Koch, ed., *Jefferson* (Englewood Cliffs, N.J.: Prentice-Hall, Inc., 1971), p. 87.

114. George Ticknor, *Life, Letters, and Journals of George Ticknor* (Boston: n.p., 1880), 1:34-35, in Koch, *Jefferson*, pp. 90-92.

115. Randall, *Life*, 3:347.

116. Isaac Jefferson, *Memoirs of a Monticello Slave, as dictated to Charles Campbell in the 1840's* (Charlottesville, Va.: University of Virginia Press, 1951), p. 27. (Hereafter referred to as *Memoirs of a Slave*.)

117. Ibid., p. 41.

118. Malone, *Jefferson the Virginian*, p. 391.

119. Adams, *Librarian*, p. 68.

120. Jefferson, "Observations on the Transportation of the Monticello Library," enclosure accompanying Jefferson to Samuel Harrison Smith, 27 February 1815, Padover, *Complete Jefferson*, pp. 1069-70.

121. Peden, "Book Collector," pp. 86, 87, citing Randall, *Life*, 1:373; 2:302; 3:337.

122. Randall, *Life*, 3:347.

123. Peterson, *New Nation*, p. 942.

124. Adrienne Koch, "Jefferson's Books—'To Nourish the Minds of American Statesmen,'" *New York Times Book Review*, 7 September 1952, p. 8. (Hereafter referred to as "Jefferson's Books.")

125. Peterson, *New Nation*, p. 943.

126. Jefferson to Adams, 10 June 1815, Cappon, *Adams-Jefferson Letters*, 2:443.

127. Koch, "Jefferson's Books," p. 8.

128. Jefferson to Adams, 10 June 1815, Cappon, *Adams-Jefferson Letters*, 2:443.

129. Lehmann, *American Humanist*, pp. 16-17.

130. Peden, "Book-Collector," pp. 157, 167.

131. Ibid., p. 167, citing Thomas Jefferson, "Account Book, 1821-1826," 13 June 1826, original, New York Historical Society, photostats, University of Virginia.

132. Jefferson, "Last Testament," 16 and 17 March 1826, Padover, *Complete Jefferson*, p. 1299.

133. Lehmann, *American Humanist*, p. 16.

134. Jefferson, *Diary*, Chinard, *Commonplace Book*, p. 2.

135. Randall, *Life*, 3:344.

136. Jefferson to Adams, 10 June 1815, Cappon, *Adams-Jefferson Letters*, 2:443.

137. Jefferson, *Preface of a Catalogue of Books Forming the Body of a Library for the University of Virginia*, Padover, *Complete Jefferson*, pp. 1091-93.

138. Jefferson to Madison, 8 August 1824, Library of Congress, Manuscript Collection, Madison Papers; in Koch, *Jefferson and Madison*, p. 279.

139. Elizabeth Cometti, *Jefferson's Ideas of a University Library* (Charlottesville, Va.: University of Virginia Press, 1950), pp. 3-13. (Hereafter referred to as *University Library*.)

140. Jefferson, *Report of a Meeting of the Visitors of the University of Virginia*, 7 October 1822, Bergh, *Writings*, 19:411-12.

141. Jefferson, *Report of a Meeting of the Visitors of the University of Virginia*, 5 March 1825, ibid., pp. 462-65.

142. Jefferson to Adams, 12 October 1823, Cappon, *Adams-Jefferson Letters*, 2:599.

143. Adams to Jefferson, 22 January 1825, ibid., p. 607.

144. Lester J. Cappon, "The Advantages of Education," *Adams-Jefferson Letters*, 2:477.

145. Ibid., pp. 477-78.

146. Jefferson, *Report of the Commissioners for the University of Virginia, meeting in Rockfish Gap*, 1-4 August 1818, Padover, *Complete Jefferson*, pp. 1097-1105.

147. Jefferson to the Trustees for the Lottery of East Tennessee College, 6 May 1810, ibid., p. 1063. See also "Jefferson's Drawings of the Buildings of the University of Virginia," ibid., p. 1099.

148. Honeywell, *Educational Work*, pp. 78-86. Honeywell gives a detailed, documented account of all steps in establishing the university by Jefferson, pp. 64-145.

149. Jefferson to Adams, 15 August 1820, Cappon, *Adams-Jefferson Letters*, 2:565.

150. Honeywell, *Educational Work*, p. 67

151. Ibid., p. 86, citing Jefferson to Madison, 24 September 1824, Bergh, *Writings*, 19:278.

152. Peden, "Book-Collector," p. 179, citing Philip Alexander Bruce, *History of the University of Virginia, 1818-1919*, 5 vols. (New York: Macmillan Co., 1920-21), 2:42.

153. Jefferson to Madison, 17 February 1826, Bergh, *Writings*, 16:155.

153. Poe to John Allan, 21 September 1826, Mary Newton Standard, ed., *Edgar Allan Poe Letters Till Now Unpublished in the Valentine Museum, Richmond, Virginia* (Philadelphia: J. B. Lippincott, 1925), pp. 43-44, in Peden, "Book-Collector," pp. 180-81.

155. Gene Gurney, *The Library of Congress* (New York: Crown Publishers, 1966), p. 9.

156. "Report of a Committee to Prepare a List of Books for Congress," 24 January 1783, Boyd, *Papers*, 6:216.

157. Peterson, *New Nation*, pp. 265-66.
158. Gurney, *Library of Congress*, p. 9.
159. Ibid., p. 10.
160. Charles A. Goodrum, *The Library of Congress* (New York: Praeger, 1974), p. 13.
161. Jefferson to Adams, 10 June 1815, Cappon, *Adams-Jefferson Letters*, 2:443.
162. Jefferson to Samuel Harrison Smith, 21 September 1814, Bergh, *Writings*, 14:191-92.
163. Jefferson to Madison, 24 September 1814, ibid., p. 196.
164. Jefferson to Monroe, 24 September 1814, Ford, *Writings*, 9: 488-89.
165. Peterson, *New Nation*, p. 943. Dr. William Thornton, Commissioner of Patents, estimated Jefferson's library to be worth at least $50,000, "but I fear . . . Congress will not give half the value," Thornton to Jefferson, 11 December 1814, in Peden, "Book-Collector," p. 147, citing William Dawson Johnston, *History of the Library of Congress, 1800-1864* (Washington: Government Printing Office, 1904), p. 79.
166. Koch, "Jefferson's Books," p. 8.
167. Ibid.
168. Gurney, *Library of Congress*, p. 11.
169. Peterson, *New Nation*, p. 943.
170. Gurney, *Library of Congress*, p. 11.
171. Adams, *Librarian*, p. 72.
172. Ibid., p. 92.
173. Adams to Jefferson, 10 February 1823, Cappon, *Adams-Jefferson Letters*, 2:587.
174. Jefferson to Adams, 25 February 1823, ibid., p. 588.
175. See, as examples, Jefferson, *Notes on Religion*, Ford, *Writings*, 2:92-103; Thomas Jefferson, *Literary Bible*, ed. Chinard; Thomas Jefferson, *Commonplace Book*, ed. Chinard.
176. Jefferson to Dr. Thomas Cooper, 10 February 1814, Bergh, *Writings*, 14:85.
177. Malone, *Jefferson the Virginian*, p. 127.
178. Peterson, *New Nation*, p. 30.
179. Lehmann, *American Humanist*, p. 11.
180. Ibid., pp. 10-11.
181. Koch, *Philosophy*, pp. xi-xiii.
182. Ibid., p. 44.
183. Adams, *Librarian*, p. 76.
184. Ibid., p. 75.
185. Ibid., p. 77. See also letter and notes, Jefferson to Ebenezer Hazard, Boyd, *Papers*, 1:164-65.
186. Adams, *Librarian*, p. 77.
187. Jefferson, *Notes on Virginia*, Bergh, *Writings*, 2:xlvi-xlvii, 1-281.
188. Jefferson, "Answers to Questions Addressed to him by Monsieur de Meusnier, author of that part of the *Encyclopedie Methodique*, entitled 'Economie Politique et Diplomatique,'" ibid., 17:49-123.

189. Jefferson, *Autobiography*, ibid., 1:1.

190. Jefferson, *The Anas*, ibid., p. 264.

191. Jefferson, *A Manual of Parliamentary Practice*, ibid., 2:333.

192. Jefferson, *The Jefferson Bible*, ibid., 20:9, 18.

193. Daniel J. Boorstin, *The Lost World of Thomas Jefferson* (New York: Henry Holt and Company, 1948), p. 194. (Hereafter referred to as *Lost World*.)

194. Stanley Pargelis, "Long Life to the Library History Round Table," *American Library History Reader*, ed. John David Marshall (Hamden, Conn.: Shoe String Press, 1961), p. 9.

195. Jefferson, *Syllabus of the Doctrines of Epicurus* and Thomas Jefferson, *Syllabus of an Estimate of the Merit of the Doctrines of Jesus, Compared with those of Others*, Bergh, *Writings*, 15:223-24, 10:381-85.

196. Jefferson to Peter Carr, 19 August 1785, 10 August 1787, Bergh, *Writings*, 5:84-87, 6:256-61.

197. Jefferson to Francis Wayles Eppes, 9 April 1822, Betts, *Family Letters*, pp. 443-44.

198. Jefferson to Thomas Mann Randolph, Jr., 27 August 1786, Ford, *Writings*, 4:290-93.

199. Ibid., pp. 444-45, and Jefferson to Peter Carr, 10 August 1787, enclosure, Boyd, *Papers*, 12:18-19.

200. Jefferson to Nathaniel Burwell, 14 March 1818, Bergh, *Writings*, 15:165-68.

201. Jefferson to Gen. Thaddeus Kosciusko, 26 February 1810, ibid., 12:369.

202. Jefferson to Madison, 1 September 1785, Jefferson to Monroe, 5 October 1781, Boyd, *Papers*, 8:460-64, 6:127.

203. Jefferson to Thomas Turpin, 5 February 1769, ibid., 1:24.

204. Jefferson to Dabney Terrell, 26 February 1821, Padover, *Complete Jefferson*, pp. 1088-90.

205. Jefferson to Dr. Thomas Cooper, 16 January 1814, Bergh, *Writings*, 14:54-59.

206. Jefferson to an unnamed friend on "studies for a lawyer," 1767, Padover, *Complete Jefferson*, pp. 1043-47.

207. Jefferson to an unnamed member of the university faculty, 25 October, 1825, ibid., pp. 1094-96.

208. Jefferson to Adams, 11 June 1812, Bergh, *Writings*, 13:156-61.

209. Enclosure, Jefferson to Robert Skipwith, 3 August 1771, Boyd, *Papers*, 1:78-81.

210. James Madison, "Report of a Committee to Prepare a List of Books for Congress," 24 January 1783, ibid., 6:216.

211. Honeywell, *Educational Work*, p. 86, citing Bruce, *History of the University of Virginia*, 2:187.

212. Johnson, *History of Libraries*, p. 319.

213. Jefferson to Samuel Harrison Smith, 21 September 1814, Bergh, *Writings*, 14:191-92.

214. Jefferson to Madison, 8 August 1824, Library of Congress,

Manuscript Collection, Madison Papers, quoted in Koch, *Jefferson and Madison*, p. 279.
215. Randall, *Life*, 3:346.
216. Jefferson to Francis Van der Kemp, 25 April 1816, Bergh, *Writings*, 15:1-3.
217. Jefferson to Adams, 25 February 1823, Cappon, *Adams-Jefferson Letters*, 2:588.
218. Ibid.
219. Randall, *Life*, 3:350.
220. Jefferson to Madison, 2 August 1787, Boyd, *Papers*, 11:662-63.
221. Sowerby, "Preface," *Catalogue*, 1:xi.
222. Sowerby, *Catalogue*, 1:4-5, 8-11, 16-17, 28-39.
223. Ibid., pp. 5, 9, 11, 16, 30-31.
224. Ibid., pp. 5, 16-17, 29-30, 37.
225. Ibid., pp. 11, 37-38.
226. Ibid., p. 9.
227. Ibid., pp. 28, 32, 36.
228. Ibid., p. 33.
229. Ibid., pp. 30, 37.
230. Ibid., pp. 32, 37, 38.
231. Ticknor, *Life, Letters, and Journals of George Ticknor*, 1:35, quoted in Koch, *Jefferson*, p. 92.
232. Adams, *Librarian*, p. 68.
233. Jefferson to Madison, 23 March 1815, Ford, *Writings*, 9:513.
234. Letter and enclosure, Jefferson to Samuel Harrison Smith, 27 February 1815, Padover, *Complete Jefferson*, pp. 1069-70.
235. Cometti, *University Library*, pp. 3-13. Jefferson did not live long enough to see the Rotunda library building entirely finished and all of the library collection in use. He did see to processing and putting to use of the books ordered from England "in the temporary library on West Lawn" where the books from Jefferson's American agent had to be stored. By September 1826 the whole library was completed and installed, one of the largest and best any university had been able to begin with; Harry Clemons, *The University of Virginia Library* (Charlottesville, Va.: University of Virginia Library, 1954), pp. 6, 10-12. (Hereafter referred to as *Virginia Library*.)
236. Jefferson to John Wyche, 19 May 1809, Bergh, *Writings*, 12:282.
237. Jefferson, "A Bill for Establishing a Public Library," Boyd, *Papers*, 2:544.
238. Jefferson, *Minutes of the Meeting of the Board of Visitors of the University of Virginia*, 5 March 1825, Bergh, *Writings*, 19:462.
239. Ibid., pp. 463-64.
240. Ibid., p. 464.
241. Jefferson to John Vaughan Kean, 1825, in Clemons, *Virginia Library*, pp. 16-17.
242. Malone, *Jefferson the Virginian*, p. 401.
243. Lehmann, *American Humanist*, p. 11.

244. Adams, *Librarian*, p. 92.
245. N.B.C. telecast, "America, the New Found Land," 14 November 1972.
246. Servies, "Bibliographic Classification," pp. 12-13.
247. Ibid., p. 13.
248. Jefferson, *Library Catalogue of 1783*, Massachusetts Historical Society, cited by Malone, *Jefferson the Virginian*, p. 401.
249. Jefferson to George Watterston, 7 May 1815, Padover, *Complete Jefferson*, p. 1,071.
250. Johnson, *History of Libraries*, pp. 23-25, 77, 122-23, 148-52.
251. Jefferson to George Watterston, 7 May 1815, Padover, *Complete Jefferson*, p. 1,071.
252. Jefferson to Judge Augustus B. Woodward, 24 March 1824, Bergh, *Writings*, 16:17.
253. Jefferson to George Watterston, 7 May 1815, Padover, *Complete Jefferson*, p. 1,071.
254. Jefferson to Judge Augustus B. Woodward, 24 March 1824, Bergh, *Writings*, 16:18.
255. Ibid.
256. See, for example, "Antient History" where editions of Josephus are numbered "J. 6, J. 7, J. 8," Thucydides' works are numbered "J. 14 through J. 17," works of Xenophon "J. 18 through 22," but "Mitford's History of Greece" is "J. 23," Sowerby, *Catalogue*, 1:4-11.
257. Jefferson to George Watterston, 7 May 1815, Padover, *Complete Jefferson*, p. 1,071.
258. Ibid., pp. 1,071-72.
259. Jefferson to Thomas Cooper, 10 July 1812, Bergh, *Writings*, 13:177.
260. Jefferson to Samuel Harrison Smith, 21 September 1814, ibid., 14:192.
261. Clemons, *Virginia Library*, p. 18.
262. Jefferson to Judge Augustus B. Woodward, 24 March 1824, Bergh, *Writings*, 16:17.
263. Melvil Dewey, *Dewey Decimal Classification and Relative Index*, 2 vols., 17th ed. (Lake Placid Club, N.Y.: Forest Press, 1965-67), 2:1,937.
264. Ibid., 1:1,104.
265. Jefferson to George Watterston, 7 May 1815, Padover, *Complete Jefferson*, p. 1,071.
266. Ibid.
267. Jefferson to Judge Augustus B. Woodward, 24 March 1824, Bergh, *Writings*, 16:18.
268. Jefferson to Dr. John Manners, 22 February 1814, ibid., 14:97-99.
269. Servies, "Bibliographic Classification," p. 100.
270. Jefferson, *Preface to a Catalogue of Books Forming the Body of a Library for the University of Virginia*, Padover, *Complete Jefferson*, p. 1,092.
271. Ibid., pp. 1,091-92.

272. Clemons, *Virginia Library*, p. 18.
273. Servies, "Bibliographic Classification," p. 2.
274. Goodrum, *The Library of Congress*, p. 15.
275. Jefferson to Madison, 24 September 1824, Bergh, *Writings*, 19:278.
276. Jefferson to James Ogilvie, 31 January 1806, Ford, *Writings*, 8:418.
277. Ibid.
278. Ibid.
279. Jefferson to Judge Augustus B. Woodward, 24 March 1824, Bergh, *Writings*, 16:18.
280. Adams, *Librarian*, pp. 93-94.
281. Servies, "Bibliographic Classification," p. 112.
282. Ibid., pp. 111-12.
283. Jefferson to unnamed correspondent, 28 September 1821, Bergh, *Writings*, 15:337-38. From the content of this letter, it seems likely Jefferson used it as a model to send to a number of officials of "colleges . . . of the South and West."
284. Jefferson expressed his concern to Madison about "the three thousand dollars duty of which we are asking the remission from Congress" for the library books purchased abroad for the University of Virginia; Jefferson to Madison, 17 February 1826, ibid., 16:155-56.
285. Jefferson to unnamed correspondent, 28 September 1821, ibid., 15:339.
286. See examples cited by Boyd in "Introduction," *Papers*, 1:1, who, along with Gilbert Chinard, calls Jefferson's papers "the richest treasure house of historical information ever left by a single man."
287. Jefferson to Adams, 10 June 1815, Bergh, *Writings*, 14:301.
288. Jefferson to Samuel H. Smith, 21 September 1814, ibid., p. 190.
289. Adams to Jefferson, 9 July 1813, Jefferson to Adams, 22 August 1813, Cappon, *Adams-Jefferson Letters*, 2:351, 368.
290. See Jefferson's concern over the power of the New England clergy to "excite . . . the public opinion" against liberal minds; Jefferson to Horatio Gates Spafford, 10 January 1816, Ford, *Writings*, 10:12-13.
291. Jefferson to Dr. Benjamin Rush, 23 September 1800, Bergh, *Writings*, 10:175.
292. Jefferson to Monsieur N. G. Dufief, 19 April 1814, ibid., 14:126-38.
293. Bestor, "Thomas Jefferson and the Freedom of Books," p. 8.
294. Jefferson to Monsieur N. G. Dufief, 19 April 1814, Bergh, *Writings*, 14:127.
295. Ibid.
296. Bestor, "Thomas Jefferson and the Freedom of Books," p. 14.
297. Ibid., pp. 15-21.
298. Ibid., p. 36.
299. Ibid., pp. 37-38.
300. Jefferson to Dr. Vine Utley, 21 March 1819, Bergh, *Writings*, 15:187.

301. Adams, *Librarian*, p. 93.
302. Ibid., p. 94.
303. Clemons, *Virginia Library*, p. 19.
304. Jefferson to Monsieur N. G. Dufief, 19 April 1814, Bergh, *Writings*, 14:127.
305. Jefferson to Dr. Benjamin Rush, 23 September 1800, ibid., 10:175.
306. Malone, *Jefferson the Virginian*, p. 285.

Notes to Chapter 3

1. Koch, *Philosophy*, p. xiii.
2. Jefferson, *Notes on Virginia*, Query 15, Bergh, *Writings*, 2:209.
3. Jefferson to John Brazier, 24 August 1819, ibid., 15:208.
4. Cousins, *In God We Trust*, p. 114.
5. Koch, *Philosophy*, p. 108.
6. William Peden, "Some Notes Concerning Thomas Jefferson's Libraries," *William and Mary Quarterly*, 3rd series, 1 (July, 1944), pp. 267-68. (Hereafter referred to as "Jefferson's Libraries.") The data and conclusions which Peden here summarizes are based on the work presented in his dissertation, Peden, "Book-Collector," pp. 15-20.
7. Peden, "Jefferson's Libraries," p. 269.
8. Jefferson to Nathaniel Macon, 12 January 1819, Ford, *Writings*, 10:120.
9. Peter Gay, *The Enlightenment: an Interpretation* (New York: Alfred A. Knopf, 1967), pp. 31-32. (Hereafter referred to as *Enlightenment*.)
10. Lehmann, *American Humanist*, p. 204.
11. Jefferson to a member of the University of Virginia faculty, 25 October 1825, Bergh, *Writings*, 16:124.
12. Sowerby lists in Jefferson's library: "Caesar, Caius Julius: *C. Julii Caesaris quae exstant* (1719), 59; (1727), 60; (French, 1708), 61, Xenophon: *De Cyri Institutione* (1727), 21; (1767), 22; *Expeditio Cyri* (1765), 19; (Eng., 1749), 20; *Graecorum Res Gestae et Agesilaus*, 18; *Hiero, sive De Regno*, 2356; *Lacedaemoniorum respublica*, 2355; *Memoirs of Socrates* and *Memorabilia*, 1307; *Oeconomica, Agesilaus, Hieron.*, etc., 2354, Thucydides: *De Bello Peloponnesiaco*, (Gr., Lat., 1731), 15; (1759), 14; *Eight Bookes of the Peloponnesian Warre*, 16, V, 16; *History of the Peloponnesian War*, 17, Diodorus Siculus: *Bibliothecae Historicae*, 37; *Historiarum*, 38, Dionysius of Halicarnassus: *Les Antiquites Romaines*, 49; *Opera Omnia Graece et Latine*, 47; *Scripta quae extant omnia*, 48, Livius, Titus: *Historiarum Libri qui extant* (1679-82), 52; (1710), 54; (Italian, 1562), 53, Tacitus, Cornelius: *Opera quae exstant*, 80; *Opera supplementis*, 81; *Works* trans. by Gordon, 80, 81; Works in Spanish, 81, Suetonius, Tranquillus, Gaius, *Opera omnia quae extant*, 82," Sowerby, *Catalogue*, 5:261, 441, 424, 248, 348, 421, 420. (Note: Sowerby gives the date of publication and the language of the edition

in parenthesis after each title and then the catalog location number for each work.)

13. Sowerby lists in Jefferson's library: "Gibbon, Edward: *History of the Decline and Fall of the Roman Empire*, 101, Segur, Louis Philippe, *History of the Principal Events of the Reign of Frederic William II, King of Prussia*, 267," Sowerby, *Catalogue*, 5:307, 410.

14. Sowerby lists in Jefferson's library: "Polybius: *Historiarum* (1619), 50; (1763, 1764), 51; (English, 1762, 1763), 51, Sallustius Crispus, Caius: *Opera omnia* (1710), 56; (1725), 58; (1746), 55; (1749), 57, Plutarch: *Ethica sive Moralia*, 1312; *Opera quae extant*, 1313; *Opuscula*, 1312; *Vitae Romanorum et Graecorum*, (1517, 1564), 68; (1572, 1774), 69," ibid., pp. 383, 408, 382.

15. Jefferson to a member of the University of Virginia faculty, 25 October 1825, Bergh, *Writings*, 16:124.

16. Ibid., p. 125.

17. Sowerby lists in Jefferson's library: "Millot, Claude Francois Xavier: *Elemens de l'Historie de France*, 189; *Elemens d'Histoire Generale, Ancienne*, 126; *Elemens . . . Moderne*, 154, Davila, Enrico Caterino, *Istoria della Guerre di Francia*, 198, Perefixe, Hardouin de Beaumont de, *Historie du Roy Henry le Grand*, 197, Sully, Maximilien de Bethune, Duc de, *Memoires*, 199, Voltaire, Francois Marie Arouet de: *Commentaire sur le livre des delits et des peines*, 2350; *Henriade*, 4297, *History of Charles XII*, 259; *Memoires pour servir a la vie de M. de Voltaire*, 221; . . . *Philosophie de l'Histoire*, 1281; *Saul*, 1283; *Oeuvres*, 4923, Marmontel, Jean Francois: *Belisarius*, 4323; *Contes Moreaux*, 4322; *Fausse Magie*, 4566; *Oeuvres posthumes*, 234; *Penelope*, 4561; *Zemire et Azor*, 4569," Sowerby, *Catalogue*, 5:361, 279, 378, 420, 433, 355.

18. Jefferson to a member of the University of Virginia faculty, 25 October 1825, Bergh, *Writings*, 16:125.

19. Sowerby lists in Jefferson's library: "Rapin, Thoyras, Paul de, *Histoire d'Angleterre*, 369, Fox, Charles James: *History of the early part of the reign of James II*, 375; *Letter to the worthy and independent electors of Westminster*, 2829; *State of the Negotiation*, 2810, Belsham, William: *History of Great Britain, from the Revolution to the Accession of the House of Hanover*, 407; *Memoirs of the Kings of Great Britain of the House of Brunswic-Lunenburg*, 408, Hume, David: *History of England*, 370, *Essays*, 1261," Sowerby, *Catalogue*, 5:395, 300, 250, 320.

20. Sowerby lists in Jefferson's library: "Russell, William: *History of Modern Europe*, 161; Robertson, William: *History of America*, 468, 469; *History of the Reign of the Emperor Charles V*, 178," Sowerby, *Catalogue*, 5:406, 404.

21. Jefferson to a member of the University of Virginia faculty, 25 October 1825, Bergh, *Writings*, 16:125-28.

22. Peden, "Jefferson's Libraries," p. 270.

23. Jefferson to Dr. Thomas Cooper, 16 January 1814, Jefferson to Dabney Terrell, 26 February 1821, Bergh, *Writings*, 14:55, 15:318.

24. Sowerby lists in Jefferson's library: "Bracton, Henry de, *De Legibus et Consuetudinitis Angliae*, 1771, Coke, Sir Edward: *Book of Entries*, 1889; *First Part of the Institutes of the Lawes of England*, 1781; *Second Part of the Institutes* (1662), 1782; (1681), 1783; *Third Part of the Institutes*, 1784; *Reports in English*, 2035; Bacon, Matthew: *New Abridgment of the Law*, 1792, Blackstone, Sir William: *Commentaries on the Laws of England* (1770), 1806; (1803), 1807; *Interesting Appendix*, 2899 and V, 2899; *Law Tracts*, 2009, *Reports of Cases*, 2081," Sowerby, *Catalogue*, 5:256, 270, 246, 254.

25. Jefferson to Dr. Thomas Cooper, 16 January 1814, Bergh, *Writings*, 14:57-59.

26. Jefferson to Madison, 17 February 1826, ibid., 16:156.

27. Jefferson to a member of the faculty of University of Virginia, 25 October 1825, ibid., 16:128-29.

28. Jefferson to Dabney Terrell, 26 February 1821, ibid., 15:319.

29. Ibid., p. 321.

30. Peden, "Jefferson's Libraries," p. 270.

31. See discussion in Koch, *Philosophy*, pp. 129-61.

32. See discussion in Boorstin, *Lost World*, pp. 171-213.

33. Jefferson to Antoine Louis Claude Destutt de Tracy, 26 January 1811, Ford, *Writings*, 9:305.

34. Jefferson to Francis Eppes, 19 January 1821, ibid., 10:183.

35. Jefferson, Catalogue of 1815, Chapter 33, p. 136, in Peden, "Jefferson's Libraries," p. 271.

36. Peden, "Jefferson's Libraries," pp. 270-71.

37. Peden, "Book-Collector," p. 65, citing Adams to Jefferson, 12 December 1816, quoted in Cappon, *Adams-Jefferson Letters*, 2:499.

38. Peden, "Book-Collector," p. 45.

39. Ibid., pp. 66-67.

40. Jefferson to Nathaniel Burwell, 14 March 1818, Bergh, *Writings*, 15:166.

41. Ibid. None of these fictitious works mentioned by Jefferson are listed in the library holdings sold to Congress; Sowerby, *Catalogue*, 5:355, 290, 306. Possibly Jefferson knew them from the reading of his granddaughters, since this letter was discussing "female education."

42. Jefferson to Robert Skipwith, 3 August 1771, Bergh, *Writings*, 4:237.

43. Ibid., pp. 238-39.

44. Randall, *Life*, 3:448-49.

45. Jefferson, *Preface to a Catalogue of Books Forming the Body of a Library for the University of Virginia*, 1820 to 1825, Padover, *Complete Jefferson*, p. 1,091.

46. Chinard, *Literary Bible*, pp. 22-30.

47. Jefferson to John D. Burke, 21 June 1801, Ford, *Writings*, 8:65.

48. Jefferson to Nathaniel Burwell, 14 March 1818, Bergh, *Writings*, 15:166.

49. Sowerby lists in Jefferson's library: "Pope, Alexander: *Iliad of*

NOTES TO CHAPTER 3

Homer, translated by Alexander Pope, Esq., 4264; *Odyssey of Homer translated by Alexander Pope, Esq.*, 4272; *Selecta Poemata Italorum*, 4384; *Verses to the Lady Mary Wortley Montague*, 3916; *Works by Warburton*, 4503; Dryden, John: *Dramatick Works*, 4543; editor and translator, Juvenal, 4487; Plutarch, 69; Virgil, 4282; Moliere, J. B. Poquelin de: *Oeuvres* (1710), 4581; (1783, 1784), 4582; Racine, Jean, *Distrest Mother*, 4555;" Sowerby, *Catalogue*, 5:383, 286, 362, 394.

50. Jefferson to Peter Carr, 19 August 1785, Bergh, *Writings*, 5:85.
51. Sowerby lists in Jefferson's library: "Terentius, Afer, Publius, *Comoediae* (1726), 4576; (1749), 4577; Theocritus: [*Opera*] *quae extant* (Gr., Lat., 1729), 4379; (1746), 4378; (Eng., 1767), 4381; (Ital., 1754), 4380; Sophocles: *Tragoediae* (Gr., Lat., 1665), 4522; (1745), 4521; (Lat., 1758), 4520; (Eng., 1758, 1759), 4523; Ossian, 101, 4377, 4452; Swift, Jonathan: Boyle, John Earl of Orrery, 383; Temple, Sir William, 366;" Sowerby, *Catalogue*, 5:422, 416, 374, 420.
52. Chinard, *Literary Bible*, p. 26.
53. Jefferson wrote of music as a "delightful recreation" for his daughters to learn and brought back a harpsichord from Europe for them. He enjoyed playing the violin. Jefferson to Nathaniel Burwell, 14 March 1818, Bergh, *Writings*, 15:167; Peterson, *New Nation*, pp. 15, 27, 343. Jefferson nowhere discussed any great ideas or themes of music as he does with books.
54. Jefferson, *Thoughts on English Prosody*, Bergh, *Writings*, 18:414-51.
55. Peden, "Book-Collector," p. 68.
56. Ibid., p. 69.
57. Lehmann, *American Humanist*, pp. 146-47.
58. Jefferson, *Thoughts on English Prosody*, Bergh, *Writings*, 18:448.
59. Randall, *Life*, 3:346.
60. Lehmann, *American Humanist*, p. 154.
61. Peden, "Jefferson's Libraries," p. 271.
62. Ibid., p. 272.
63. Peterson, *New Nation*, p. 30.
64. Jefferson to Peter Carr, 19 August 1785, Bergh, *Writings* 5:87; Jefferson to Francis Eppes, 13 December 1820, Betts, *Family Letters*, p. 437.
65. Jefferson, *Farm Book*, in Peterson, *New Nation*, pp. 528-32.
66. Isaac Jefferson, *Memoirs of a Slave*, p. 8.
67. Ibid., p. 27.
68. Jefferson to Dr. Thomas Cooper, 10 July 1812, Bergh, *Writings*, 13:176.
69. Cyrus Adler, "Jefferson as a Man of Science," in Bergh, *Writings*, 19:p. vii. (Hereafter referred to as "Man of Science.")
70. Peterson, *New Nation*, pp. 159-60.
71. Jefferson, *Autobiography*, Appendix Note G. "Summary of own Achievements," Bergh, *Writings*, 1:256-58.
72. Peterson, *New Nation*, pp. 46-49.

73. Jefferson to Dr. Benjamin Waterhouse, 3 March 1818, Bergh, *Writings*, 15:164-65.

74. Adler, "Man of Science," p. x.

75. Peden, "Book-Collector," p. 20.

76. Ibid., p. 21.

77. Ibid.

78. Sowerby studied the printed catalog produced by George Watterston for the Library of Congress, Jefferson's handwritten catalog, and searched early sources to verify entries; Sowerby, *Catalogue*, 1:xi. She had to be something of a detective, Koch relates, since most of Jefferson's original volumes had been damaged by fire or changed by new bindings or endpapers; Koch, "Jefferson's Books," p. 8.

79. Merrill D. Peterson, *The Jefferson Image in the American Mind* (New York: Oxford University Press, 1960), p. 432. (Hereafter referred to as *Jefferson Image*.)

80. Jefferson to George Watterston, 7 May 1815, Padover, *Complete Jefferson*, p. 1,071.

81. Jefferson to Elbridge Gerry, 26 January 1799, Bergh, *Writings*, 10:78.

82. Jefferson to Samuel Harrison Smith, 21 September 1814, ibid., 14:191-92.

83. Jefferson to Dr. Peter Wilson, Professor of Languages, Columbia College, N.Y., 20 January 1816, Bergh, *Writings*, 14:402.

84. Jefferson, *Essay on the Anglo-Saxon Language*, ibid., 18:359-411.

85. Jefferson, *Indian Addresses*, ibid., 16:370-472.

86. Jefferson to Dr. Thomas Cooper, 16 January 1814, ibid., 14:60.

87. Worthington Chauncy Ford, "Introduction, the John Quincy Adams Library," in *A Catalogue of the Books of John Quincy Adams Deposited in the Boston Athenaeum*, ed. Henry Adams (Boston: Athenaeum, 1938), pp. 4-6.

88. Adams to Jefferson, 2 March 1816, Cappon, *Adams-Jefferson Letters*, 2:464. See also Cappon's comments on "the contrast between the tall, angular, . . . reserved Jefferson and the chubby, rotund, . . . humorous Adams," ibid., 1:xxxvi.

89. Jefferson to Adams, 8 April 1816, ibid., 2:467.

90. See Peterson's discussion of the contribution of Jefferson to American theory of democracy and society through the ideas expressed in the Declaration of Independence; Peterson, *Jefferson Image*, pp. 304-308.

91. Adams to Jefferson, 22 September 1813, Jefferson to Adams, 12 October 1813, Cappon, *Adams-Jefferson Letters*, 2:378-86.

92. Adams to Jefferson, 9 July 1813, ibid., 2:350.

93. Cappon, "Introduction," ibid., 1:xlvii. .

94. James Truslow Adams, *The Founding of New England* (Boston: Little, Brown and Co., 1933), pp. 369-70.

95. Morrison argues that Adams was misled by some early "inaccurate" studies in *William and Mary Quarterly* instead of following the "authoritative analysis" in P. A. Bruce, *Institutional History of*

Virginia in the Seventeenth Century (1910), 1:402-41; Morrison, *The Intellectual Life of New England*, p. 133.

96. Ibid., pp. 32-42, 46-48, 52, 105-106, 113, 115.
97. Ibid., pp. 55-56.
98. Thomas Edward Keys, "Private and Semi-private Libraries of the American Colonies" (Master's thesis, University of Chicago, 1934), pp. 73-77.
99. Peden, "Book-Collector," pp. 3, 12.
100. William Byrd, *The London Diary (1717-1721) and Other Writings*, ed. by Louis B. Wright and Marion Tinkling (New York: Oxford University Press, 1958), p. 19.
101. See Adams's disgusted comments after reading the letters of a French courtesan, Mademoiselle De Lespinasse; Adams to Jefferson, 13 February 1819, Cappon, *Adams-Jefferson Letters*, 2:533.
102. Adams to Jefferson, 18 July 1813, ibid., pp. 361-62.
103. Jefferson to Adams, 22 August 1813, ibid., p. 369.
104. See the version of the New Testament that Jefferson's interest in the moral teachings of Jesus led him to edit; Jefferson, *The Life and Morals of Jesus of Nazareth*, Bergh, *Writings*, 20:402-516.
105. Jefferson replied to one of Adams's speculations, "When I meet with a proposition beyond finite comprehension, I abandon it as I do a weight which human strength cannot lift"; Jefferson to Adams, 14 March 1820, Cappon, *Adams-Jefferson Letters*, 2:562.
106. Jefferson to Thomas Jefferson Randolph, 24 November 1808, Bergh, *Writings*, 12:197-98.
107. Johnson, *History of Libraries*, p. 319.
108. Johnson, *History of Libraries*, p. 319.
109. Ibid., p. 318.
110. Peden, "Book-Collector," pp. 130-31, citing Jefferson to N. G. Dufief, 4 February 1803, 1 March 1803, Library of Congress, *Jefferson's Papers*, A.L.S.
111. Edwin Wolf, "Franklin and His Friends Choose Their Books," *An American Library History Reader*, ed. John David Marshall, (Hamden, Conn.: Shoe String Press, 1961), p. 21.
112. Chinard, *Literary Bible*, pp. 82-151.
113. Jefferson to Samuel Harrison Smith, 21 September 1814, Bergh, *Writings*, 14:191-92.
114. Cousins, *In God We Trust*, p. 114.
115. Koch, *Philosophy*, pp. 106-107.
116. Boorstin, *Lost World*, pp. 23-24.
117. Lehmann, *American Humanist*, p. 204.
118. Jefferson to George Watterston, 7 May 1815, Padover, *Complete Jefferson*, p. 1,071.
119. Jefferson to Samuel Harrison Smith, 21 September 1814, Bergh, *Writings*, 14:191.
120. Jefferson to an unnamed member of the University of Virginia faculty, 25 October 1825, ibid., 16:124.
121. Jefferson to Nathaniel Burwell, 14 March 1818, ibid., 15:166.

122. Chinard, *Literary Bible*, pp. 72-140.
123. Jefferson to John Brazier, 24 August 1819, Bergh, *Writings*, 15:208-209.
124. Jefferson, *Autobiography*, ibid., 1:3-4.
125. Lehmann, *American Humanist*, pp. 51-53.
126. See Adler, "Man of Science," Bergh, *Writings*, 19:iii-x.
127. Jefferson to Timothy Pickering, 27 February 1821, Bergh, *Writings*, 15:323-24.
128. See Adams to Jefferson, 12 May 1820, Jefferson to Adams, 15 August 1820, in which Jefferson wrote, "Your crowd of scepticisms on matter, spirit, motion, etc. . . . kept me from sleep," Cappon, *Adams-Jefferson Letters*, 2:563-69, 567.
129. Adams to Jefferson, 10 March 1823, Jefferson to Adams, 11 April 1823, ibid., 2:590-94.

Notes to Chapter 4

1. According to a conversation with Jefferson's grandson reported in Thomas Jefferson Randolph to Henry S. Randall, Randall, *Life*, 3:674.
2. Jefferson's daughter Martha said that her father "would not give up a friend or an opinion," Randall, *Life*, 1:384.
3. Leonard W. Levy, *Jefferson and Civil Liberties: the Darker Side* (Cambridge, Mass.: Harvard University Press, 1963), pp. 161-63, blames Jefferson's "willfulness."
4. See Jefferson's citations arguing for the moral obligations of treaties to President Washington, Jefferson, *Opinion on the Question whether the United States have a Right to Renounce their Treaties with France*, Bergh, *Writings*, 3:235-39.
5. See discussion in Peterson, *Jefferson Image*, pp. 92-98, 127-30, 243, 302-304.
6. See the biased attack by J. Leslie Hall, "The Religious Opinions of Thomas Jefferson," *The Swanee Review*, 21, no. 2 (April, 1913):164-76.
7. Jefferson to Adams, 22 August 1813, Cappon, *Adams-Jefferson Letters*, 2:369.
8. Sowerby, *Catalogue*.
9. Jefferson to Judge Augustus B. Woodward, 24 March 1824, Bergh, *Writings*, 16:19.
10. Jefferson to Peter Carr, 7 September 1814, ibid., 19:215.
11. Koch, *Philosophy*, pp. xiii, ix-x.
12. Melvil Dewey, *Dewey Decimal Classification and Relative Index*, 2 vols., 17th ed. (Lake Placid Club, N.Y.: Forest Press, 1965-67), 1:112-13.
13. See Jefferson's use of quotations from these authors in Jefferson, *Opinion on the Question whether the United States have a Right to Renounce their Treaties with France*, 28 April 1793, Bergh, *Writings*, 3:235-39.

14. Ernst Troeltsch, "The Enlightenment," *The New Schaff-Herzog Religious Encyclopedia,* 13 vols (Grand Rapids, Mich.: Baker Book House, 1952), 4:144.
15. Sowerby, *Catalogue,* 1:1-20, 32.
16. Ibid., pp. 28-38.
17. Jefferson to Mrs. Anne Carey Bankhead, 8 December 1800, in Sowerby, *Catalogue,* 1:38.
18. Sowerby, *Catalogue,* 1:46-50, 31.
19. Ibid., p. 16.
20. Ibid., pp. 286-93.
21. See Jefferson to Jared Sparks, 4 November 1820, Bergh, *Writings,* 15:288; Jefferson to Adams, 15 August 1820, Cappon, *Adams-Jefferson Letters,* 2:568.
22. Sowerby, *Catalogue,* 1:293.
23. Ibid., pp. 295-96.
24. Ibid., pp. 293-94.
25. Ibid., p. 296.
26. Jefferson to Adams, 14 October 1816, in Sowerby, *Catalogue,* 2:3.
27. Jefferson to Adams, 14 March 1820, Cappon, *Adams-Jefferson Letters,* 2:562; Jefferson to Adams, 15 August 1820, ibid., pp. 567-69.
28. Sowerby, *Catalogue,* 2:5-8, 27-28, 45, 52.
29. Ibid., pp. 23-25.
30. Ibid., pp. 10-16, 21-23, 47.
31. Anthony Ashley Cooper, Earl of Shaftesbury, *Characteristicks of Men, Manners, Opinions, Times,* Ford, *Writings,* 2:95.
32. Jefferson to Timothy Pickering, 27 February 1821, Bergh, *Writings,* 15:34; Jefferson to Charles Thomson, 29 January 1817, Ford, *Writings,* 10:76, Jefferson, *Notes on Virginia,* Ford, *Writings,* 3:263-64.
33. Chinard, *Commonplace Book,* pp. 278-81, 383.
34. Jefferson, *Notes on Virginia,* Ford, *Writings,* 3:263-65; Jefferson to Horatio G. Spofford, 17 March 1814, Bergh, *Writings,* 14:119; Jefferson, "A Bill for Establishing Religious Freedom," Ford, *Writings,* 2:237-38.
35. Jefferson, *Notes on Religion,* Ford, *Writings,* 2:102-103.
36. See discussion in Chinard, *Commonplace Book,* p. 41; Peterson, *New Nation,* p. 94; and Malone, *Jefferson the Virginian,* p. 227.
37. Jefferson to Peter Carr, 10 August 1787, Ford, *Writings,* 4:429-30.
38. Ernst Troeltsch, "Deism," *The New Schaff-Herzog Encyclopedia of Religious Knowledge,* 1958, 3:391-92.
39. Jefferson to Francis W. Gilmer, 7 June 1816, Bergh, *Writings,* 15:24-25; Jefferson to Adams, 14 October 1816, ibid., p. 76.
40. Jefferson to Adams, 25 December 1813, ibid., 14:34.
41. Chinard, *Literary Bible,* pp. 40-41, 48-50, 54-55.
42. Ibid., pp. 60-61.
43. Jefferson to Ezra Styles, 25 June 1819, Bergh, *Writings,* 15:203; Jefferson to James Fishback, 27 September 1809, ibid., 12:315.
44. Jefferson to Adams, 11 April 1823, ibid., 15:426.

45. See Troeltsch, "Deism," p. 393.

46. Jefferson to Timothy Pickering, 27 February 1821, Bergh, *Writings*, 15:323; Jefferson to James Smith, 8 December 1822, ibid., p. 409.

47. Sowerby, *Catalogue*, 2:21, note on Title 1280.

48. See discussion in Chinard, *Commonplace Book*, pp. 44, 48-49, 63.

49. Jefferson had copies of the *Encyclopédie Méthodique*, *Works of Aristotle*, *Works of Cicero*, *Works of Bacon*, and *Works of John Locke* in the reference section of his library labeled "Polygraphical" works; Sowerby, *Catalogue*, 5:143-69.

50. See discussion of Jefferson's scientific writings on American wildlife for Frenchmen by Stuart Gerry Brown, *Thomas Jefferson* (New York: Washington Square Press, 1966), pp. 38-39.

51. Sowerby, *Catalogue*, 2:14-26.

52. Jefferson to Adams, 8 April 1816, Cappon, *Adams-Jefferson Letters*, 2:467.

53. Jefferson to Adams, 8 April 1816, Bergh, *Writings*, 14:469.

54. See the many terms for God compiled from Jefferson's writings by Robert M. Healey, *Jefferson on Religion in Public Education* (Hamden, Conn.: Shoe String Press, 1970), pp. 27-28.

55. Jefferson to Adams, 11 April 1823, Bergh, *Writings*, 15:426-27.

56. Chinard, *Literary Bible*, pp. 58-59.

57. Chinard, *Commonplace Book*, pp. 331-32.

58. Randall, *Life*, 3:346.

59. Sowerby, *Catalogue*, 2:28-33.

60. Ibid., pp. 34-41.

61. Ibid., pp. 39-43.

62. See passages Jefferson copied as his favorites; Chinard, *Literary Bible*, pp. 17, 72, 93, 102, 120, 172, 189.

63. According to Chinard, ibid., p. 18.

64. Jefferson, *Syllabus of the Doctrines of Epicurus*, enclosed in Jefferson to William Short, 31 October 1819, Bergh, *Writings*, 15:223-24.

65. Jefferson to William Short, 31 October 1819, ibid., p. 221.

66. Lehmann, *American Humanist*, pp. 71, 156-59, 177-87.

67. Jefferson to Joseph Priestley, 9 April 1803, Ford, *Writings*, 8:224-25.

68. Jefferson to Dr. Benjamin Rush, 21 April 1803, Bergh, *Writings*, 10:381-82.

69. Sowerby, *Catalogue*, 2:32-33.

70. Jefferson to William Short, 4 August 1820, Bergh, *Writings*, 15:258.

71. Jefferson to Adams, 12 October 1813, ibid., 13:388.

72. Ibid., pp. 390-91.

73. Bolingbroke, *Philosophical Works*, as excerpted by Jefferson in Chinard, *Literary Bible*, pp. 45-46, 57, 64, 68-70.

74. Sowerby, *Catalogue*, 2:27, 44, 16-17, 53-54.

75. Ibid., pp. 22, 45-51.

76. Ibid., pp. 53-56.

77. Jefferson to Brissot de Warville, 12 February 1788, Bergh, *Writings*, 6:428.

78. Jefferson, *Autobiography*, Bergh, *Writings*, 1:34-35, 72-73.

79. Jefferson, *Notes on Virginia*, Bergh, *Writings*, 2:191-92, 197-200, 225-27; Jefferson, *Answers to Questions of Monsieur de Meusnier, author of that part of the Encyclopédie Méthodique, entitled Economie Politique et Diplomatique*, Bergh, *Writings*, 17:98-99, 103.

80. Note by Jefferson written in his copy of Henry Home, Lord Kames, *Essays on the Principles of Morality and Natural Religion*, p. 147, in Sowerby, *Catalogue*, 2:11-12.

81. Jefferson to Judge Augustus B. Woodward, 24 March 1824, Bergh, *Writings*, 16:19.

82. Sowerby, *Catalogue*, 2:67-72.

83. Jefferson, *Opinion on the Question of Whether the United States have a Right to Renounce their Treaties with France*, 28 April 1793, Bergh, *Writings*, 3:235-41.

84. Sowerby, *Catalogue*, 2:70-74.

85. Jefferson to Peter Carr, 10 August 1787, Bergh, *Writings*, 6: 257; Jefferson to Adams, 14 October 1816, ibid., 15:76; Jefferson to Thomas Law, 13 June 1814, ibid., 14:142; Jefferson to Francis W. Gilmer, 7 June 1816, Ford, *Writings*, 10:32.

86. Jefferson to James Fishback, 27 September 1809, Bergh, *Writings*, 12:315; Jefferson to Adams, 5 May 1817, ibid., 15:109.

87. Sowerby lists in Jefferson's library: "Law, Thomas: *Ballston Springs*, 4453; *Second Thoughts on Instinctive Impulses*, 3250; *Thoughts on Instinctive Impulses*, 3250," Sowerby, *Catalogue*, 5:341.

88. Jefferson to Thomas Law, 13 June 1814, Bergh, *Writings*, 14:138.

89. Randall, *Life*, 3:344-45.

90. Randall commented, "His petit-format library, contained in four cases, was each . . . between three and four feet in width and height and were . . . of the smallest sized editions. He had first made this collection for his convenience at Washington." Ibid.

91. Jefferson to Thomas Law, 13 June 1814, Bergh, *Writings*, 14:139.

92. Ibid., p. 144.

93. Ibid., p. 141.

94. Isaac Jefferson, *Memoirs of a Slave*, pp. 27-38.

95. Sowerby, *Catalogue*, 2:70-74.

96. Ibid., pp. 91-97.

97. Jefferson to Charles Thomson, 25 December 1808, Bergh, *Writings*, 12:217.

98. Sowerby, *Catalogue*, 2:98-103.

99. Ibid., pp. 98-99.

100. Randall, *Life*, 1:17, 41.

101. Jefferson to Thomas Jefferson Smith, 21 February 1825, Ford, *Writings*, 10:340-41.

102. Jefferson to Adams, 12 October 1813, Cappon, *Adams-Jefferson Letters*, 2:380-81.

103. Sowerby, *Catalogue*, 2:107-110.

104. Jefferson to Peter Carr, 10 August 1787, Bergh, *Writings*, 6:261.
105. Sowerby, *Catalogue*, 2:107-108.
106. Ibid., pp. 111-12.
107. Ibid., pp. 106-107.
108. Ibid., pp. 105-106.
109. Jefferson to Rev. William Pryce, 15 October 1803, in ibid., p. 105.
110. Jefferson to Dr. Joseph Priestley, 29 January 1804, Bergh, *Writings*, 10:445-46.
111. Sowerby, *Catalogue*, 2:104-105.
112. Jefferson to Dr. Joseph Priestley, 29 January 1804, Bergh, *Writings*, 10:446.
113. Ibid.
114. Cyrus Adler, "Introduction to the Jefferson Bible," in Bergh, *Writings*, 20:10-11.
115. Jefferson to Dr. Joseph Priestley, 29 January 1804, Bergh, *Writings*, 10:446.
116. Jefferson to Adams, 22 August 1813, Cappon, *Adams-Jefferson Letters*, 2:368.
117. Jefferson to Dr. Benjamin Rush, 21 April 1803, Bergh, *Writings*, 10:379-80; Jefferson to Adams, 22 August 1813, ibid., 13:351-52; Jefferson to William Short, 13 April 1820, ibid., 15:243.
118. Sowerby, *Catalogue*, 2:124, 89-90.
119. Ibid., pp. 171-75.
120. Ibid., pp. 130-31.
121. Ibid., p. 130.
122. Ibid., pp. 125-29, 131-34.
123. Ibid., pp. 126-30, 185-88.
124. "Joseph Priestley," *The New Schaff-Herzog Encyclopedia of Religious Knowledge*, 1957, 9:254.
125. Sowerby, *Catalogue*, 2:119-123.
126. Jefferson to Henry Fry, 17 June 1804, in ibid., p. 120.
127. Jefferson to Adams, 22 August 1813, in ibid.
128. Sowerby, *Catalogue*, 2:119-20.
129. "Conyers Middleton," *The New Schaff-Herzog Encyclopedia of Religious Knowledge*, 1956, 7:365.
130. Jefferson to Peter Carr, 10 August 1787, Ford, *Writings*, 4:429-32; Jefferson to Adams, 22 August 1813, ibid., 9:408-18.
131. Jefferson to William Ludlow, 6 September 1824, Bergh, *Writings*, 16:75; Jefferson to Adams, 12 September 1821 and 4 September 1823, ibid., 15:334, 465.
132. Jefferson to Adams, 22 August 1813, Ford, *Writings*, 9:418.
133. Jefferson to Dr. Joseph Priestley 9 April 1803, Bergh, *Writings*, 10:374-75; Jefferson to Jared Sparks, 4 November 1820, ibid., 15:288; Jefferson to James Smith, 8 December 1822, ibid., 15:408-409.
134. Jefferson to Adams, 15 August 1820, Cappon, *Adams-Jefferson Letters*, 2:568.
135. Jefferson to F. A. Van Der Kemp, 25 April 1816, Bergh, *Writings*, 15:2-3; Jefferson to Dr. Joseph Priestley, 9 April 1803, and 29 January

1804, ibid., 10:374-75, 445-46; Jefferson to William Short, 13 April 1820 and 4 August 1820, ibid., 15:244, 259.

136. Jefferson to Adams, 11 April 1823, Cappon, *Adams-Jefferson Letters*, 2:593-94.

137. Sowerby, *Catalogue*, 2:113-15.

138. Ibid., pp. 116, 191, 163-64.

139. Randall, *Life*, 3:555.

140. Sowerby, *Catalogue*, 2:142-48, 191.

141. Jefferson to Adams, 15 August 1820, Cappon, *Adams-Jefferson Letters*, 2:568.

142. Sowerby, *Catalogue*, 2:116, 127, 133-34.

143. Jefferson to Dr. Benjamin Waterhouse, 26 June 1822, Bergh, *Writings*, 15:384, for example.

144. Jefferson to Adams, 11 April 1823, ibid., p. 425.

145. Chinard, *Commonplace Book*, pp. 332-33.

146. Sowerby, *Catalogue*, 2:124-26, 132-35, 159, 165.

147. Ibid., pp. 126-27.

148. Ibid., pp. 126, 128-30.

149. Ibid., pp. 127-31, 149, 151, 154, 158, 164.

150. Ibid., pp. 125, 129, 149, 151-52, 155, 160-61, 188.

151. Chinard, *Literary Bible*, pp. 15-18.

152. Sowerby, *Catalogue*, 2:150.

153. Ibid., pp. 152-53.

154. Ibid., pp. 162, 168-69, 190-91.

155. Ibid., pp. 191.

156. Ibid., pp. 167, 189-90.

157. See Jefferson, *Notes on Virginia*, Ford, *Writings*, 3:261-66; Jefferson, "A Bill for Establishing Religious Freedom," ibid., 2:237-39.

158. Sowerby, *Catalogue*, 2:44.

159. Jefferson, *Notes on Religion*, Ford, *Writings*, 2:92-103.

160. Sowerby, *Catalogue*, 2:156-60, 165.

161. Sowerby, note to work by Toussaint, ibid., p. 157.

162. See Jefferson to Thomas Jefferson Randolph, 24 November 1808, in which Jefferson advises, "Politeness is . . . the practice of sacrificing to those whom we meet in society, all the little conveniences." Bergh, *Writings*, 12:198.

163. Sowerby, *Catalogue*, 2:134-41.

164. Ibid., pp. 134-41, 166-69, 182, 187.

165. Ibid., pp. 175-76, 178, 180-81, 183-84, 186-87, 155.

166. Ibid., pp. 134-41, 149, 178.

167. Ibid., pp. 137, 179.

168. Ibid., pp. 141, 149, 171, 185.

169. Ibid., pp. 155, 166-67, 175, 179, 186.

170. In Sowerby, *Catalogue*, 2:182, Title 1687.

171. Ibid., p. 177.

172. Ibid., pp. 140, 170, 177-78, 181-84, 186, 189.

173. Ibid., pp. 376-77, 379, 382-83.

174. Ibid., pp. 378-79.

175. Ibid., pp. 377, 379.

176. Ibid., pp. 378-79.

177. Jefferson, *Notes on Virginia*, Ford, *Writings*, 3:261-66.

178. Jefferson, *Autobiography*, Ford, *Writings*, 1:52-55.

179. Jefferson, *Notes on Religion*, Ford, *Writings*, 2:101-102.

180. Jefferson to Dr. Thomas Cooper, 10 February 1814, Bergh, *Writings*, 14:85-97; Jefferson to Adams, 24 January 1814, ibid., 14:72-75; Jefferson to Major John Cartwright, 5 June 1824, ibid., 16:42-44, 48-51.

181. Sowerby, *Catalogue*, 2:224, 28.

182. Jefferson to Adams, 11 April 1823, Cappon, *Adams-Jefferson Letters*, 2:592.

183. Jefferson to Adams, 22 August 1813, Ford, *Writings*, 9:408-18.

184. Jefferson to Thomas Law, 13 June 1814, Bergh, *Writings*, 14:138-44.

185. See the account of the attacks upon Jefferson's religion during the presidential campaign of 1800. Dumas Malone, *Jefferson and the Ordeal of Liberty* (Boston: Little, Brown and Co., 1962), p. 479.

186. Jefferson to Dr. Benjamin Rush, 21 April 1803, Bergh, *Writings*, 10:379-80.

Notes to Chapter 5

1. Peden, "Book-Collector," p. 183.

2. Jefferson to Adams, 17 May 1818, Cappon, *Adams-Jefferson Letters*, 2:524.

3. Jefferson to Dr. Vine Utley, 21 March 1819, Bergh, *Writings*, 15:187.

4. Jefferson to Thomas Turpin, 5 February 1769, Boyd, *Papers*, 1:24.

5. Randall, *Life*, 3:344.

6. Jefferson to Adams, 10 June 1815, Cappon, *Adams-Jefferson Letters*, 2:443.

7. Jefferson to Samuel H. Smith, 21 September 1814, Bergh, *Writings*, 14:191-92.

8. Ibid.

9. Sowerby, *Catalogue*.

10. Ibid., 1:xi.

11. Servies, "Bibliographic Classification," p. 2.

12. Jefferson to Adams, 15 June 1813, Cappon, *Adams-Jefferson Letters*, 2:332.

13. Jefferson to Adams, 12 September 1821, ibid., p. 575.

14. Jefferson to Adams, 11 April 1823, Cappon, *Adams-Jefferson Letters*, 2:591.

15. Jefferson to Mrs. M. Harrison Smith, 6 August 1816, Bergh, *Writings*, 15:60.

16. Jefferson to Adams, 11 April 1823, Cappon, *Adams-Jefferson Letters*, 2:591-92.

17. See Jefferson's *Notes on Religion*, Ford, *Writings*, 2:92-103, in which Jefferson quotes and comments on his readings from early Christian heresies, "Locke's system of Christianity," Shaftesbury's *Characteristicks*, Milton on the episcopacy, and Locke on *Toleration*.

18. See Jefferson's discussion of authors and ideas on the moral law in Jefferson to Thomas Law, 13 June 1814, Bergh, *Writings*, 14:138-44.

19. Jefferson to Adams, 5 July 1814, ibid., pp. 147-50.

20. Randall, *Life*, 3:672, quoting the recollections of Jefferson's grandson given in Thomas Jefferson Randolph to Henry S. Randall.

21. Ibid.

22. Jefferson to William Short, 21 October 1819, Bergh, *Writings*, 15:219-20.

23. Jefferson, *Syllabus of an Estimate of the Merit of the Doctrines of Jesus, Compared with those of Others*, ibid., 10:384.

24. Jefferson to Adams, 12 October 1813, ibid., 13:388.

25. Ibid., pp. 389-90, and also Jefferson to William Short, 21 October 1819, ibid., 15:221.

26. Peden, "Book-Collector," p. 91.

27. Peden, "Jefferson's Libraries," p. 272.

28. Peterson, *New Nation*, p. 724. Source of quotation not given.

29. Peterson, *Jefferson Image*, p. 9.

30. Ibid., p. 14.

Selected Bibliography

I. Collections of Jefferson's Writings

Cappon, Lester J., ed. *The Adams-Jefferson Letters.* 2 vols.
Chapel Hill, N.C.: University of North Carolina Press,
1959.

Jefferson, Thomas. *The Commonplace Book of Thomas Jefferson: a Repertory of His Ideas on Government.* Edited
by Gilbert Chinard. Baltimore: Johns Hopkins Press,
1926.

————. *The Complete Jefferson.* Edited by Saul K. Padover.
New York: Duel, Sloan, and Pearce, 1943.

————. *The Family Letters of Thomas Jefferson.* Edited
by Edwin Morris Betts and James Adams Bear, Jr. Columbia, Mo.: University of Missouri Press, 1966.

————. *A Jefferson Profile.* Edited by Saul K. Padover. New
York: John Day Co., 1956.

————. *The Literary Bible of Thomas Jefferson: His Commonplace Book of Philosophers and Poets.* Edited by Gilbert
Chinard. New York: Greenwood Press, 1969.

————. *The Papers of Thomas Jefferson.* Edited by Julian
P. Boyd. 17 vols. Princeton: Princeton University Press,
1950-65.

————. *The Writings of Thomas Jefferson.* Edited by Albert
Ellery Bergh. 20 vols. Washington, D.C.: The Thomas
Jefferson Memorial Association, 1907.

_____ . *The Writings of Thomas Jefferson.* Edited by Paul Leicester Ford. 10 vols. New York: G. P. Putnam's Sons, 1892-98.

II. *Monographs on Jefferson's Libraries and Reading Interests and Contemporary Libraries and Reading Interests*

Adams, Henry, ed. *A Catalogue of the Books of John Quincy Adams Deposited in the Boston Athenaeum.* Boston: Athenaeum, 1938.

Adams, James Truslow. *The Founding of New England.* Boston: Little, Brown and Co., 1933.

Adams, Randolph Greenfield. *Three Americanists: Henry Harrisse, Bibliographer; George Brinley, Book Collector; Thomas Jefferson, Librarian.* Philadelphia: University of Pennsylvania Press, 1939.

Bestor, Arthur. "Thomas Jefferson and the Freedom of Books." *Three Presidents and Their Books.* Urbana, Ill.: University of Illinois Press, 1955.

Byrd, William. *The London Diary (1717-1721) and Other Writings.* Edited by Louis B. Wright and Marion Tinkling. New York: Oxford University Press, 1958.

Byrd, William. *The Writings of Colonel William Byrd in Virginia.* Edited by John Spencer Bassett. New York: Doubleday, Page and Co., 1901.

Clemons, Harry. *The University of Virginia Library.* Charlottesville, Va.: University of Virginia Library, 1954.

Cometti, Elizabeth. *Jefferson's Idea of a University Library.* Charlottesville, Va.: University of Virginia Press, 1950.

Goodrum, Charles A. *The Library of Congress.* New York: Praeger, 1974.

Gurney, Gene. *The Library of Congress.* New York: Crown Publishers, 1966.

Hart, James D. *The Popular Book: a History of America's Literary Taste.* New York: Oxford Press, 1950.

Johnson, Elmer. *History of Libraries in the Western World.* 2d ed. Metuchen, N.J.: Scarecrow Press, 1970.

Keep, Austin Baxter. *The Library of Colonial New York.* New York: Burt Franklin, 1970.

Keys, Thomas Edward. "Private and Semi-private Libraries of the American Colonies." Master's thesis, University of Chicago, 1934.

Krause, Joe Walker. "Book Collections of Five Colonial College Libraries: A Subject Analysis." Ph.D. dissertation, University of Illinois, 1960.

Morrison, Samuel Elliot. *The Intellectual Life of Colonial New England*. Ithaca, N.Y.: Cornell University Press, 1965.

Peden, William Harwood. "Thomas Jefferson: Book-Collector." Ph.D. dissertation, University of Virginia, 1942.

Servies, James Albert. "Thomas Jefferson and His Bibliographic Classification." Master's thesis, University of Chicago, 1950.

Shera, Jesse H. *Foundations of the Public Library: The Origins of the Public Library Movement in New England, 1629-1855*. Hamden, Conn.: Shoe String Press, 1965.

Sowerby, E. Millicent, comp. *Catalogue of the Library of Thomas Jefferson*. 5 vols. Washington, D.C.: Library of Congress, 1952-59.

III. Monographs on Jefferson and His Beliefs

Boorstin, Daniel J. *The Lost World of Thomas Jefferson*. New York: Henry Holt and Co., 1948.

Brown, Stuart Gerry. *Thomas Jefferson*. New York: Washington Square Press, 1966.

Cousins, Norman. *In God We Trust: The Religious Beliefs and Ideas of the American Founding Fathers*. New York: Harper Brothers, 1958.

Foote, Henry Wilder. *Thomas Jefferson: Champion of Religious Freedom, Advocate of Christian Morals*. Boston: Beacon Press, 1947.

Gay, Peter. *The Enlightenment: An Interpretation*. New York: Alfred A. Knopf, 1967.

Healey, Robert M. *Jefferson on Religion in Public Education*. Hamden, Conn.: Shoe String Press, 1970.

Honeywell, Roy J. *The Educational Work of Thomas Jefferson*. New York: Russell and Russell, 1964.

Jefferson, Isaac. *Memoirs of a Monticello Slave as Dictated to*

Charles Campbell in the 1840's. Charlottesville, Va.: University of Virginia Press, 1951.

Koch, Adrienne, ed. *Jefferson.* Englewood Cliffs, N.J.: Prentice-Hall, Inc., 1971.

————. *Jefferson and Madison.* New York: Alfred A. Knopf, 1950.

————. *The Philosophy of Thomas Jefferson.* Gloucester, Mass.: Peter Smith, 1957.

Lehmann, Karl. *Thomas Jefferson: American Humanist.* Chicago: University of Chicago Press, 1965.

Malone, Dumas. *Jefferson and His Time.* Vol. 1: *Jefferson the Virginian.* Vol. 2: *Jefferson and the Rights of Man.* Vol. 3: *Jefferson and the Ordeal of Liberty.* Vol. 4: *Jefferson the President, First Term, 1801-1805.* Vol. 5: *Jefferson the President, Second Term, 1805-1809.* Boston: Little, Brown and Co., 1948-74.

Peterson, Merrill D. *The Jefferson Image in the American Mind.* New York: Oxford University Press, 1960.

————. *Thomas Jefferson and the New Nation.* New York: Oxford University Press, 1970.

Randall, Henry Stephens. *The Life of Thomas Jefferson.* 3 vols. New York: Derby and Jackson, 1858.

Rosenberger, Francis Coleman, ed. *Jefferson Reader.* New York: E. P. Dutton and Co., 1953.

Schulz, Constance Bartlett. "The Radical Religious Ideas of Thomas Jefferson and John Adams: A Comparison." Ph.D. dissertation, University of Cincinnati, 1973.

Trainer, M. Rosaleen. "Thomas Jefferson on Freedom of Conscience." Ph.D. dissertation, St. John's University, 1966.

Williams, Kenneth Raynor. "The Ethics of Thomas Jefferson." Ph.D. dissertation, Boston University, 1962.

IV. *Articles and Other Materials on Jefferson, Contemporary Thought, and Library History*

Adler, Cyrus. "Jefferson as a Man of Science." *The Writings of Thomas Jefferson.* Edited by Albert Ellery Bergh. Washington, D.C.: The Jefferson Memorial Association, 1907. Vol. 19:iii-x.

————. "The Jefferson Bible." *The Writings of Thomas Jefferson.* Edited by Albert Ellery Bergh. Washington, D.C.: The Thomas Jefferson Memorial Association, 1907. Vol. 20:404-90.

Bryan, William Jennings. "The Statute for Establishing Religious Freedom." *The Writings of Thomas Jefferson.* Edited by Albert Ellery Bergh. Washington, D.C.: The Thomas Jefferson Memorial Association, 1907. Vol. 8:i-xi.

"Conyers Middleton." *The New Schaff-Herzog Encyclopedia of Religious Knowledge.* Grand Rapids, Mich.: Baker Book House, 1956. Vol. 7:365.

Cooke, Alistair. "America, the New Found Land." N.B.C. telecast, 14 Nov. 1972.

Cooledge, Thomas Jefferson. "Jefferson in His Family." *The Writings of Thomas Jefferson.* Edited by Albert Ellery Bergh. Washington, D.C.: The Thomas Jefferson Memorial Association, 1907. Vol. 15:i-vii.

Ford, Worthington Chauncy. "Introduction, the John Quincy Adams Library." *A Catalogue of the Books of John Quincy Adams Deposited in the Boston Athenaeum.* Edited by Henry Adams. Boston: Athenaeum, 1938.

Gottschick, Johannes Friedrich. "Natural Law." *The New Schaff-Herzog Encyclopedia of Religious Knowledge.* Grand Rapids, Mich.: Baker Book House, 1956. Vol. 8: 83-86.

"Joseph Priestley." *The New Schaff-Herzog Encyclopedia of Religious Knowledge.* Grand Rapids, Mich.: Baker Book House, 1956. Vol. 9:254.

Koch, Adrienne. "Jefferson's Books—'To Nourish the Minds of American Statesman.'" *New York Times Book Review,* 7 Sept. 1952, pp. 8-9.

Pargellis, Stanley. "Long Life to the Library History Round Table." *American Library History Reader.* Edited by John David Marshall. Hamden, Conn.: Shoe String Press, 1961.

Peden, William Harwood. "Some Notes on Jefferson's Libraries." *William and Mary Quarterly,* 3rd series, 1 (July, 1944):265-72.

Shores, Louis. "Importance of Library History." *American*

Library History Reader. Edited by John David Marshall. Hamden, Conn.: Shoe String Press, 1961.

Troeltsch, Ernst. "Deism." *The New Schaff-Herzog Encyclopedia of Religious Knowledge.* Grand Rapids, Mich.: Baker Book House, 1952. Vol. 3:391-96.

——— . "The Enlightenment." *The New Schaff-Herzog Encyclopedia of Religious Knowledge.* Grand Rapids, Mich.: Baker Book House, 1952. Vol. 4:141-47.

Wolf, Edwin. "Franklin and His Friends Choose Their Books." *American Library History Reader.* Edited by John David Marshall. Hamden, Conn.: Shoe String Press, 1961.

Index

Adams, John: character contrasted with Jefferson's, 98-99, 102-103; comments on Jefferson's newspaper file, 50; deplores book burning and censorship, 73; discusses religion with Jefferson, 125, 129; educated in the classics, 100; enjoys reading novels, 85, 98-99; interest in art, 100, 112; interest in classical literature, 100, 112; interest in fiction, 98-99; interest in history, 98, 112; interest in law, 98; interest in literature, 98, 112; interest in philosophy, 100-101, 113; interest in politics, 98; interest in religion, 101-103, 113; interest in science, 100, 112; Jefferson discusses reading with, 22-23; library of (*see* Library of John Adams); praises Jefferson for establishing University of Virginia, 44; told by Jefferson of his newspaper file, 56

Adams, John Quincy: library of, 98

Addison, Joseph, 84

Adler, Cyrus, 131

Admiralty law, 83. *See also* Law, maritime

Aeschines Socraticus, 124

Aeschylus: Jefferson's interest in, 85, 89

Age of Reason (Paine), 135

Agriculture. *See* Farming

Alembert, Jean Le Rond D', 123

Alexander of Aphrodisius, 124

Alexandrian library, 73

Allen, Ethan, 121

Americana, 93, 96

American Indians. *See* Indians, American

Anabaptist sect, 131, 134

Anacreon, 87

Ancient history: Enlightenment interest in, 81; Jefferson's interest in, 81-82, 96, 111, 119; Jefferson's library holdings in, 80-82, 119, 139

Ancient libraries. *See* Libraries, ancient

Anglo-Saxon: langauge, 97; law, 50; people and institutions admired by Jefferson, 86

Antonius, Marcus Aurelius, 124

Apocalypse: Jefferson's library holdings in books of, 131, 136
Aopcrypha, 129, 140
Appianus of Alexandria, 119
Aquinas, St. Thomas, 90
Architecture: Jefferson's interest in, 97, 112; Jefferson's library holdings in, 94. *See also* Jefferson, Thomas, architect for
Aristotle: *Ethica*, 124
Arnet, Peter, 121
Art: Ben Franklin's interest in, 106; Jefferson believes ladies should study, 32; Jefferson believes libraries should foster, 36; Jefferson's classification of, 65, 66; Jefferson's interest in art, 87, 97, 100, 112, 124, 146; Jefferson's interest in music, 87-88, 97, 112, 146; Jefferson's lack of artistic temperament, 87-88; Jefferson's lack of interest in painting, 87-88, 97; Jefferson selects books in for a personal library, 55; Jefferson selects books in for University of Virginia Library, 55; John Adam's interest in, 100; William Byrd's interest in, 104
Ashurbanipal: library of at Ninevah, 61
Athanasius, 120
Atheism: attacks on Jefferson over, 122; influence on Jefferson of, 122, 140, 149; Jefferson's explanation of, 123; library holdings of Jefferson on, 122-23; of Calvin, 134
Austin, David, 137

Bacon, Francis: classifies all learning by "tree of knowledge", 64-65, 66, 67, 71, 116-118; Enlightenment influence of on Jefferson, 25, 92, 147, 149; Jefferson's library holdings of, 121; provides Jefferson with his library classification scheme,

38, 60, 62; provides Philadelphia Company Library with library classification scheme, 61
Baldwin, Abraham, 105
Baptist associations, 137. *See also* Anabaptist sect
Batteux, Charles, 125
Baxter, Andrew: *The Nature of the Human Soul*, 121
Bayle, Pierre, 122
Beckley, John James, 47
Bede, Venerable, 90; *History of the Church of England*, 120
"Belle-lettres". *See* Fiction; Literature
Bentham, Jeremy, 83
Bible: Commentaries in Jefferson's library, 130, 140; Jefferson's "Bible," 130-31, 151; Jefferson's interest in, 90, 120, 128-131, 135, 138, 140, 151; Jefferson a student of, 130-31, 142, 157; laws not part of civil law, 139;
Bibliophile: George Ticknor as, 41; Jefferson as true, 151-54; Jefferson has Milton first editions, 85; Jefferson not enthusiastic as, 29; Jefferson's preference for scholarly to special editions, 49; Jefferson uses first editions for study, 57-58
Bibliothèque Nationale, 62
Biographical Chart (Priestley), 26
Biography: lack of use of classification by Jefferson, 99; John Adam's interest in, 98-99; popular libraries holdings in, 107
Bishops, 119-20
Blackstone, Sir William, *Commentaries on the Laws of England*, 74-75, 83
Bland, Colonel Richard: Jefferson purchases his library, 25; member of Congressional library committee consulted by Jefferson, 36, 46
Blount, Charles, 121

142, 149; influences Jefferson to an interest in science, 96, 113; inspires Jefferson to create his own library, 24-25; inspires Jefferson to seek encyclopedic knowledge, 24-25, 51; and intellectual freedom, 73-75, 147-48; interest in classifying knowledge, 66-67, 70-71, 116-18; interest in comparative religions, 131, 151; interest in history, 81; Jefferson as foremost American leader of, 113; Jefferson recommends Enlightenment books to his nephew and grandson, 30-31; of mankind is God's purpose according to Jefferson, 36; moral law idea of, 127, 140; new basis of ethics and society, 118; and religious freedom, 73-75; should be spread to all the people according to Jefferson, 34-35, 147-48

Enquiry Concerning Political Justice (Godwin), 83
Epictetus, 124
Epicurean philosophy: influence on Jefferson, 124, 140
Epicurus, 124
Episcopal Church: established position in Virginia, 138-39; Jefferson's interest in, 129, 133, 134, 140, 150; Jefferson's sermons by clergy of, 136
Epistemology: Jefferson's belief about, 121; Jefferson's library holdings in, 121
Essays on the Principles of Morality and Natural Religion (Kames), 126
Essay on the Principles of Population (Smith), 83
Ethica (Aristotle), 124
Ethics: basis of courtesy, 135, 150; basis of international law, 115; basis of law and society, 126-28, 140, 142, 150; Jefferson approves only of fiction that teaches an

ethical lesson, 85-86, 88, 112; Jefferson's belief in duty, 150; Jefferson's classification of, 116-18; Jefferson deplores French immorality, 27; Jefferson's interest in Greek and Roman moral philosophers, 123-25, 140; Jefferson's interest in the study of, 18, 21; Jefferson recommends study of, 30-31; Jefferson selects books on for libraries, 55; Jefferson's sermons on, 136; Jefferson writes essays on, 54; must include education and enlightenment according to Jefferson, 36
Ethics and Morals (Plutarch), 124
Euripides, 87, 89
Eusebius, Pamphilius, 119, 133

Fabricius, Johann Albert, 129-30
Farming: Jefferson's interest in, 19, 90-92, 147
Felice, Fortunatio, 127
Feudal system, 86
Fiction: authors approved by Jefferson, 84-90; Ben Franklin's lack of interest in, 106; Jefferson opposes reading of, 32, 85; Jefferson wants it to teach a moral lesson, 85-86, 88; John Adam's interest in, 98-99; not in Jefferson's library, 79, 112; public libraries' interest in, 106, 112; William Byrd's interest in, 103
Fielding, Henry, 84
Florus, Lucius Annaeus, 119
Foreign Languages: Ben Franklin's lack of interest in, 106; Jefferson's fluency in, 80; William Byrd's interest in, 103
France: French Revolution, 127; Jefferson as American minister to, 46, 128; Jefferson collects books there, 20, 26, 27, 41, 45, 56, 138; Jefferson collects scandals of kings of, 58; Jefferson educates daughters in French convent, 30;

character as seen by John F. Kennedy, 153; character as seen by later scholars, 153-54; character as seen from his reading, 151-54; contribution to librarianship, 49, 60-61, 68, 71, 145-46, 151-54; his "commonplace" college notebooks (see "Commonplace" notebooks of Thomas Jefferson); death beliefs, 23-24; education in youth, 17-19; educated in classics, 17-19, 80-81, 100, 112; educated in law, 18, 126-27; educated at William and Mary College, 80; embargo policy explained by his reading interests, 115; as an "encyclopedist", 51, 115, 122, 145; frontier influence upon, 96; influence on history, 153-54; as a librarian, 42, 49-52, 75-78, 93, 110-11, 145-46. 151-52, (see also Librarian, circulation; Librarian, reference; Librarianship; Librarian and technical processing; Library cataloguing; Library classification; Library, reference; Library regulations; Reader's advisory service); his library (see Library of Thomas Jefferson); praises his father, 18-19; as a philosopher, 51; as a philosophé, 51; presidential administration of as extended by Madison and Monroe, 29; reading discussed with John Adams and Thomas Law, 22-23, 127-28; gives reading advice to John Adams and others, 22-23, 27-32, 54, 146 (see also Reader's advisory service); encourages reading and book collecting by his grandchildren, 20, 24; reading interests (see Reading interests of Thomas Jefferson); religion of (see Religion of Thomas Jefferson); retirement life, 20-24, 31, 145, 152; slanders against, 50, 126, 128, 140; slavery opinions,

126; as statesman, 127-28; study enthusiasm, 18-20, 42, 50-52, 114, 115, 127-28, 134, 145, 146, 148, 152; in Washington's cabinet, 127

Jesus Christ: "harmonies" about, 130-31; Jefferson's theological library holdings about, 134, 136; Jefferson's view of, 124, 133, 141; Jefferson's writings about, 53, 54, 130-31; moral doctrines of emphasized by Jefferson, 130-31, 151; as moral teacher, 133, 151; his teachings "corrupted", 133; resurrection of studied by Jefferson, 130, 134

Jews: Jefferson's aversion to ethics of, 125, 131

John Adams' library. See Library of John Adams

Josephus, Flavius, *Works*, 119

Justin Martyr, 133

Justinus, Marcus Junianus, 119

Kames, Lord, (Sir Henry Home), 121; *Essays on the Principles of Morality and Natural Religion*, 126; influence on Jefferson's ethics, 128, 142, 149

Kant, Immanuel, 125

Kennedy, John F.: estimate of Thomas Jefferson, 153

King Lear (Shakespeare), 86

Knighthood: and Scott's novels, 86

Knowledge: Bacon's classification of by faculties and "tree of", 64-67; importance of libraries in promoting, 36-37; Jefferson deplores suppression of, 73; Jefferson's interest in classifying, 66-67; Jefferson's pursuit of, 18, 20-22, 50-52; libraries as depositories of, 11-12, 72, 144; "light of", 147-48

Knox, John, *The Historie of the Reformation of the Church of Scotland*, 120

Koran, 90, 131

Lackington, James, 26
Lafayette, General Marquis de, 34
Latin: Jefferson's Bibles in, 128-29,
131, 140; Jefferson's reading in,
80, 119, 133, 139; Vulgate Bible,
128
Latin classics: Jefferson's fondness
for, 85, 88-90, 100; Jefferson's
library holdings in, 85, 112;
Jefferson recommends, 87; John
Adams's interest in, 100
Law: Anglo-Saxon studied by Jefferson, 50; Ben Franklin's lack of
interest in, 105; books in first
Library of Congress, 46; importance of books for the study of,
30; Jefferson advises grandson
how to study, 31; Jefferson advises Thomas Cooper how to
teach, 31; Jefferson's comments
on study of, 83; Jefferson's plan
for the study of, 30; Jefferson's
study of, 18, 138; Jefferson's study
of reflected by extensive library
holdings, 62, 66, 82-83, 95, 111,
138, 146, 150; John Adams' interest in, 98; William Byrd's interest
in, 104. See also Admiralty law;
International law; Law ecclesiastical; Law maritime; Law
merchant
Law, church. See Law, ecclesiastical
Law, common. See Common law
Law, ecclesiastical: importance of
in early America, 138-39; Jefferson's library holdings in, 94,
138, 141, 142, 150; for marriage
and divorce, 138; study of, 83
Law, international. See International law
Law, maritime, 94. See also
Admiralty law
Law, merchant, 94
Law, religious. See Law, ecclesiastical
Law, Thomas, *Second Thoughts
on Instinctive Impulses,* 127

Le Beau, Charles, 119
Letter Concerning Toleration
(Locke), 121, 135
Librarian, circulation: Jefferson
as, 58-60, 69-70, 77, 146
Librarian, reference: Jefferson's
activities as, 52-54, 77, 97, 146
Librarianship: influence of Jefferson upon through his influence
upon the Library of Congress,
49; Jefferson called "father of
American", 60; Jefferson's contribution to through work in
cataloging and classifying
books, 60-61, 68, 71; Jefferson's
importance in, 78, 93, 144-46;
151-52; Jefferson's interest in,
49-52, 144; problem of censorship and Jefferson's solution,
73-75
Libraries: as depositories for
human knowledge, 11-12, 72,
144, 151-54; destruction of
deplored by Jefferson and
Adams, 72-73, 77-78, 152. *See
also* Librarianship; Libraries,
ancient; Libraries, college and
university; Libraries, medieval;
Libraries, social; Library cataloguing; Library classification;
Library of Congress; Library,
county system; Library and
historical research; Library
history, Library, public; Library
reference; Library regulations;
Library and society; Library,
technical processes; School
libraries; University of Virginia
library
Libraries, ancient: burning of
deplored by Jefferson and
Adams, 73; classification of
clay tablets, 61; Roman cataloging of, 62
Libraries, college and university:
early American college libraries,
107-110; early American college
libraries compared with Jeffer-

JEFFERSON AND HIS LIBRARY

Library regulations: devised by Jefferson for University of Virginia Library, 43-44, 59-60, 77; of Jefferson for use of his library, 69-70, 77; proposed by Jefferson for early Virginia libraries, 36-37, 58-59

Library of Rhode Island College. *See* Rhode Island College Library

Library of Smithsonian Institution, 131

Library and Society: effect on democracy, 74-75; mutual interaction, 12-15, 153-54; records of society, 72, 144, 151-52; social change, 12-15, 144

Library technical processes: Jefferson's interest in, 17, 20; Jefferson processes books of University of Virginia's library, 43, 45-46; Jefferson processes his own library, 56-58, 77, 146; Jefferson processes and packs his library to send to Library of Congress, 58; Watterston processes Jefferson's library at Library of Congress, 49; William Byrd hires librarian for, 56

Library of Thomas Jefferson: books from it loaned by Jefferson to friends, 38; carefully processed by Jefferson, 56-58, 146; catalogue of published by Library of Congress for Jefferson's bicentenniel, 93; Chastellux's description of, 39; compared with contemporary college libraries, 148; compared with contemporary popular libraries, 148; compared with Harvard College library, 110; compared with John Adams,' 98-103, 113, 141; compared with William Byrd's, 103-104; description of by A. Koch, 41-42; description of Jefferson's library rooms, 39-

41; description of retirement library formed after main library sold to Congress, 41, 42, 145; evaluation of, 97, 110; first to be classified by subject instead of size, accession order, or author, 60-61, 64, 76; George Ticknor's description of, 39; his "petit-format" traveling one, 42-43, 127, 145; his three libraries, 80, 145; Isaac Jefferson's description of, 40, 91; Jefferson's description of, 38-39, 69-70; Jefferson forms his first, 25, 37; Jefferson's grandson's description of, 39-40; Jefferson makes first catalogue in 1783, 36, 38; Jefferson starts second after first burns, 25, 37; reveals his intellectual interests and character, 79-80, 115-16, 145-46, 148; shows his interest in study and good literature, 79-80, 146-47; sold by Jefferson for Library of Congress, 37, 40-41, 47-48, 58, 145; used by Jefferson to educate young men, 31, 55

Library of Thomas Jefferson, holdings: in Apocalpse, 131; in Aopcrypha, 129; in art, 87-88, 94, 97, 99, 100, 112; in Bible, 90, 120, 128-31, 135, 138, 140, 151; in church history, 119-20, 133, 139; in ethics, 120-28, 140; in fiction, 84-86, 97, 98, 112; in history, 80-82, 96, 98, 111, 119-20; in law, 82-83, 95, 98, 111, 126-27, 138; in philosophy, 120-26, 139-40; in poetry, 87-89, 97; in politics, 83-84, 95, 98, 111; in prayer book and catechism, 133, 138, 140, 141, 150; in reference books, 97-98; in religion, 90, 95, 113, 115-39, 148-51; in science, 90, 96, 100, 109, 113; in sermons, 136-38, 141; in theology, 125, 134-8, 140-41, 148-50.

Minucius, Felix Marcus, 124
Miscellaneous Works (Middleton), 132
Missionary Societies, 137
Molière, J. B. Poquelin de, 87
Monroe, James: consulted by Jefferson about sale of library to congress, 48; extends Jefferson's administration, 29; Jefferson advises him on books, 29; Jefferson guides his education, 29-30
Montaigne, Michel Eyquem de, 122
Montesquieu, C.L. de Secondat, 83; *Spirit of Laws*, 74, 84
Monticello: agriculture at, 90-92; emulates a Roman villa, 112-13, 124; Jefferson builds library for, 58, 91, 145; Jefferson builds with slaves, 19; Jefferson's library rooms at, 38-41, 69-70; visited by Ticknor, 39; visited by Chastellux, 19
Moral Admonitions (Cato), 124
Morality. *See* Ethics
Moral law: Jefferson's belief in, 126-28, 140, 142, 149, 150
Moral Tales (Marmontel), 86
Moravian sect, 131, 134
More, Sir Thomas, *Utopia*, 83
Music: Jefferson's interest in, 87-88, 97, 112, 146; Jefferson recommends its study by women, 32
Mysticism: Jefferson's aversion to, 150

Napoleonic Wars, 115, 147
Natural Science. *See* Science
The Nature of the Human Soul (Baxter), 121
Nelson, John, 91
New England: 101-103, 113, 136
A New History of the Holy Bible . . . (Stackhouse), 120
Newspapers: Jefferson's interest in reading, 21, 81; Jefferson

keeps file in his library, 50, 56
New Testament: harmony of, 130-31, 151; Jefferson's library holdings of, 90, 128-29, 135, 140, 151; Jefferson publishes article on, 56; Jefferson's study of, 20, 128-31, 140, 151; Jefferson writes books on 53, 151
Newton, Isaac: Enlightenment influence on Jefferson, 25, 92, 147, 149; need not be defended by censorship according to Jefferson, 74
New York Public Library, 12
New York State Society Library, 46
Ninevah, 61
No Cross, No Crown (Penn), 131
Norman customs, 86
Novels: approved by Jefferson, 85-86; John Adams' interest in reading, 98-99; of Scott disapproved by Jefferson, 86. *See also* Fiction; Literature

Old Testament: Jefferson's aversion to laws of, 124-25; Jefferson's library holdings of, 128-30; Jefferson studies Daniel, 131; Jefferson studies Job and Isaiah and Psalms, 129
Ore, Billy, 9
Origen, 133
Origin of the Cults (Dupuis), 125
Ossian: Jefferson's enthusiasm for his poems, 19, 87; Jefferson recommends reading, 87

Paine, Thomas: *Age of Reason*, 135; Jefferson's opinion of, 84
Palmer, Elihu, 121
Paradise Lost (Milton), 87
Paschale, Chronicon, 119
Peel, Joshua, 121
Penn, William, *No Cross, No Crown*, 131
Philadelphia Company Library: early cataloging and classifica-

rational instead of based on faith, 122, 140, 149; skeptical of miracles, 122, 129; and slavery, 126, 137, 150; studies sects, 131-32; Unitarian influence, 122, 142, 149. *See also* Religion, Religious freedom

Religious Freedom: and censorship, 73-75, 77-78; and church establishment, 65, 135, 150; collaboration of Jefferson and Madison in working for, 29; and ecclesiastical law, 65, 138-39, 150; Enlightenment struggle for, 73, 81, 122-23, 147; Jeffersons concern for, 77-78, 121, 127, 135, 138-39, 140; Jefferson's library holdings about, 121, 135, 138-39, 141

Rhode Island College Library: holdings in classics, 109; holdings in law, government, politics, 110; holdings in literature, 109, 112; holdings in science, 109; holdings in theology, 109. *See also* Table 8, 108

Roman: life influences Jefferson, 112-13, 124; pagan influences on Christianity, 131; religions, 131

Roman Libraries. *See* Libraries, ancient.

Roman Literature. *See* Classical literature

Rudiments of the Faith (Calvin), 134

Rush, Benjamin, 131

Saavedra, Miguel de Cervantes, *Don Quixote*, 85
Saint Augustine, *Confessions*, 133
Saint Gregory of Nazianzus, 133
Saint Ignatius, 133
School Libraries, 34
Schools. *See* Education
Science: Ben Franklin's interest in, 100, 105, 110, 113; importance

to human progress of, 36; Jefferson's interest in, 18, 31, 62, 90-93, 96, 100-103, 110-11, 113, 146-47; Jefferson's interest in natural, 66-67, 111; John Adams' interest in, 100; William Byrd's interest in, 104

Scott, Sir Walter, 86
Second Thoughts of Instinctive Impulses (Law), 127
Sects, religious, 131-32, 134
Seneca, Lucius Annaeus, 124, 131
A Sentimental Journey through France and Italy (Sterne), 85
Separation of church and state, 138-39, 141
Septuagint Bible, 128-29
Sermons (Bourdaloue), 136
Sermons (Clarke), 136
Sermons (Tillotson), 136
Shadwell, 25
Shaftesbury, Lord (Anthony Ashley Cooper), 121
Shakespeare, William: Jefferson's interest in his plays, 18, 86; Jefferson's library holdings of, 84, 112; *King Lear*, 86; *Macbeth*, 86
Short, Willaim (Jefferson's former secretary), 23
Skipwith, Robert, 28-29
Slavery, 126, 137, 150
Small, William, 18, 24, 25
Smith, Adam, *Inquiry into the Nature and Causes of the Wealth of the Nations*, 83
Smith, Samuel Harrison, 47
Smithsonian Library. *See* Library of Smithsonian Institution
Social change: and Enlightenment, 92; and libraries, 13-15
Social Science: Jefferson's interest in, 84, 92, 95, 99-100, 111, 142, 146. *See also* Political Science
Society: ethical basis of, 126-27, 140, 142, 150; importance to of fostering education, 34-35, 147;